Mr. McGuire: I want to say one word to you. Just one word.

Benjamin: Yes, sir.

Mr. McGuire: Are you listening?

Benjamin: Yes, I am.

Mr. McGuire: Plastics.

Benjamin: Exactly how do you mean?

Mr. McGuire: There's a great future in plastics. Think about it. Will you think about it?

—*Walter Brooke (Mr. McGuire) and Dustin Hoffman (Benjamin) in the classic 1967 film* The Graduate

SALES FIRST!
Growing Our Company the Old-Fashioned Way

The ColorMatrix Story

John Haugh &
Michael Shaughnessy

with Becca Braun

The Braun Collection
Cleveland

Produced and published by Braun Ink as part of the Braun Collection—executive biographies and memoirs for a business professional, business student, and general audience. Additional formats and companion products are available. For further information, see www.braunink.com or contact info@braunink.com

ISBN: 978-1-7355999-0-8
VI.3

I dedicate this book to all the hard-
working employees of ColorMatrix.
—John

I dedicate this book to the memory
of my late wife, Marian, who
inspired me to build ColorMatrix.
—Mike

Contents

Introduction 11

FOUNDING

1. Rosemar of Ohio 15
2. Liquid Color 18
3. Makeshift Lab 22
4. What's Terracotta? 25
5. Opportunity Seekers 28
6. SALES FIRST! 31
7. Long Live SALES FIRST! 34
8. Learning to Sell 38
9. Sales Rep 40
10. Angel Customers 43
11. A Pretty Riotous Guy 45
12. Walking a Tightrope 47
13. Things Fall Apart 49
14. Lack of Goodwill 51
15. The FBI Raid 54
16. Our 50-50 Partnership 58
17. Like Brothers 61
18. Making Decisions 65

19. Beers at the Holiday Inn 71
20. Polyetheylene Terepthalate 73
21. Great Relationships 75
22. Liquid Carbon Black 77
23. Clubs, Airplanes 80
24. Coca-Cola 84
25. Glossy Flyers 87
26. Solutions Selling 90
27. Goal: $100 Million 105
28. European Partners 107
29. Opportunists 109
30. Great Partners 112
31. Entering Asia 114
32. South America 117
33. TripleA Scavenger 119
34. Amosorb 123
35. See You at the Top 128
36. Working Smarter 131
37. Improving Quality 133
38. Adding Depth 136
39. Employee Assistance 139
40. Workforce Development 143
41. Enablers? 147
42. City Hall 150
43. Bye, Cleveland 153
44. Dark Cloud 158

45. Leveraged Recap 163

46. I-Bankers 166

47. How Big Companies Think 168

48. Sellers' Anxiety 172

49. Panic Attack 176

50. String of Successes 179

51. Growth Drivers 182

52. A Global Enterprise 185

53. Ready to Sell 190

54. Gray 193

Postscript 196

Introduction

When we started ColorMatrix, an entrepreneurial venture in colorants, we had a lot going against us. As Midwesterners with chemistry degrees and few business contacts, we had no training in entrepreneurship and only cursory knowledge of colorants. We also hardly had two nickels to rub together and knew nothing about finance or how to raise money—a couple more strikes against us. We set up our business in Cleveland, a Rust Belt town with a lagging economy, dilapidated buildings, and a largely unskilled workforce.

How can you successfully grow a company when you are two inexperienced chemists at a geographic disadvantage with no money and few contacts?

This book answers that question, but here's a preview: We knew something about plastics and operations, which meant we understood our customers' needs and could make a product that worked for them. We aggressively sold and marketed, turning customer opportunities into sales. This was how we raised money for growth—not from venture capitalists but from customers. We called it our SALES FIRST! approach. And we had fantastic mentors and partners. We openly recognized, in the moment, that a string of people helped us: our parents, bosses, customers, clergy, and friends.

Ours is not an iconic, high-drama story of success created by incredibly smart, well-connected people. We never had a breakthrough idea or a moment of clarity when we knew success would be ours. We didn't quit our jobs to start a company that would make us rich. As middle managers at big companies, we possessed the scrappy desire to be our own bosses, and we had mentors who gave us the chance to do this. When we struck out on our own, we had a total commitment to hunting down every opportunity presented to us, as if each one was a winning lottery ticket we were cashing in. We saw how commercially important color was becoming and knew how to make color effective, efficient, and successful for our customers.

If you aren't important, seasoned, wealthy, or well-connected, but you want to be a successful entrepreneur, this book is for you. It's a how-to manual dressed up as a timeless story. Our biggest issue with entrepreneurship as it's taught today is too many people think they need a breakthrough invention, an Ivy-League education, wealthy parents, or venture capital investors to be successful entrepreneurs. Great if you've got it, but hardly necessary. The ColorMatrix story will show that you can still be your own boss, change the world, create jobs, build a valuable company, and make great money.

—*John Haugh and Mike Shaughnessy*
Cleveland, Ohio 2014

PART I

Founding

CHAPTER I

Rosemar of Ohio

MIKE

When I consider all the times I've made connections and grown my business, my mind immediately turns to driving. During my second post-college job as a regional sales representative for Cincinnati Milacron, I steered my company-issued, green Ford Torino around places like Toledo, Cleveland, Youngstown, and Akron, selling heat stabilizer for use in polyvinyl chloride (PVC) applications.

In the early 1980s, after John and I had teamed up and become independent sales reps selling liquid and solid additives to plastics processors on behalf of Synpro, we drove our beat-up cars on the Ohio River Valley's narrow roads, taking in the rolling green hills and fog-shrouded valleys while meeting our plastic company clients.

During one of these drives, John and I came across three businessmen in Chicago who owned a fledgling company called Rosemar Industries. Knowing we were experts in functional additives for cutting-edge polymers, these Chicagoans wanted to talk with us about liquid colorant.

"These guys claim they've developed a liquid colorant for PVC," John said.

"We're thinking you might add it to your bag of tricks when you're out meeting with plastics companies," a Rosemar guy said.

The Rosemar guys knew their stuff, and they convinced us that liquid colorant was likely to take share from dry (or powdered) colorant and become a big business. John and I liked the opportunity Rosemar outlined and became very interested in selling its new liquid colorant to the plastics industry.

"The problem is," one of them added, "we're a very small business and can't pay you much, if anything."

Being scrappy and opportunistic, we agreed to a classic start-up compensation structure that involved equity ownership. We would establish a new entity, Rosemar Industries of Ohio ("Rosemar of Ohio"). We would own a controlling stake in that entity, and the three Chicago businessmen would own a significant minority stake. John and I now had two businesses: Chemiplast, our repping business through which we sold the Synpro line, and Rosemar of Ohio, our new liquid colorants company, a business that would generate precious little near-term revenue.

In fact, we had to set up Rosemar of Ohio's manufacturing capability, which required capital investment and personnel. We found a windowless, 200-square-foot, single-car garage behind a hardware store at East 140th Street and Lakeshore Boulevard in Cleveland and made that our laboratory and pilot plant. We set our headquarters address as John's condominium because that's where we did our billing.

Chemiplast became the cash cow for the mini-conglomerate we were building because, in the best scenario, no cash would come from our Rosemar of Ohio work for at least six months—four months to turn a prospect into a customer, and then two months to invoice and receive payment.

We could have scrambled to secure angel investors for Rosemar, but investors would have created a board of directors. The board likely would have controlled the company's future, making John and me hard-working employees of an investor-run company rather than decision makers in our own business. We hadn't left Cincinnati Milacron to report to a board of directors; we had left so we could be our own men.

We generated enough cash through our repping business to reinvest in Rosemar of Ohio. Having Chemiplast as our ATM is one of the most important structures we established in all our years of doing business.

If we hadn't had this second revenue stream as we were building Rosemar of Ohio, we never would have made it financially. We and our families needed the steady cash flow Chemiplast provided to finance our foray into the new and unproven liquid colorant realm.

Initially, Chemiplast brought in 95 percent of our income and Rosemar the rest. As partners in two businesses, John and I were like brothers. Although we didn't bring to the table a Rolodex of venture capital investors, we did respect and listen to each other, and we shared the same vision for hunting down opportunities, selling our products, and growing our companies.

CHAPTER 2

Liquid Color

JOHN

I, too, always loved the scenery of the Rust Belt because it represented opportunity. As I drove through towns like Parkersburg, West Virginia, and Ironton, Ohio, I passed through an area that had the largest concentration of plastics processors in the world, and I knew none of them would survive if they didn't improve their operations. During World War II, big-company researchers had devised dozens of new plastic and resin formulations. The result was that plastics processors then needed the capability of processing dozens of resins with specific combinations of strength, resilience, heat tolerance, and recyclability.

To do this, small processors on the outskirts of worn-down towns had to invest in specialized equipment. Yet this was a time, in the 1980s, when a massive tsunami of competition was coming on the scene: for every dollar a U.S. worker got paid, a Chinese one got paid three cents. Hong Kong, Taiwan, the Philippines, Thailand, Japan, and India had similar workforce dynamics.

"The only way our Rust Belt customers have a fighting

chance is to wring out every single unnecessary cost in the entire supply chain," I often said to Mike.

We knew they needed to invest in equipment and teach floor supervisors to use it efficiently. For them, our liquid colorants represented a new and better way to add color to plastic. Plastics processors were at the time using color pellets and powders instead of liquid. They poured clear plastic resin into a hopper, added color pellets, and melted and mixed them together until the resin reached the targeted uniform color.

Depending on the type of plastic, they sometimes dried the newly colored resin to lower its moisture content. When they switched to a different product on the same manufacturing line, a worker had to clean the hopper and equipment, and then load a new resin, all of which created excess downtime. The cleaning process also had safety issues: Workers at the feed throat of the hopper usually stood atop ladders or on raised platforms.

At other times, processors pre-mixed the resin with color in an area away from the processing line in a separate back room. That way, the processor didn't have to do the mixing in the hopper on the line. Still other processors purchased pre-mixed color ("pre-color") resins, which had to be kept in inventory. Pallets of different-colored resins, instead of just one clear resin, usurped warehouse space.

Compared to these three powder and pellet options, our liquid colorant was less expensive, more efficient, and safer. It required no hopper for melting and mixing because it came, by definition, in liquid form. Instead, it dispensed *in process*. Using a small, attached dispensing system, a line worker, process engineer, or colorist pre-set the color dispenser and fed the liquid colorant into clear resin while it was moving through the injection molding or extrusion press.

"You just need to turn on the dispensing system," I said to executives when I demonstrated it, turning the dial as they watched. "That's it. It's that simple."

Liquid colorant also had higher pigment ratios than concentrate pellets, so plastics processors needed a much smaller amount of our colorant, compared to pellets and powders, to reach the right color. I could go into the executives' warehouses and show them the fraction of storage space needed for liquid color versus solid color concentrate.

When we first came across liquid colorant, Mike and I quickly recognized these benefits, yet we could drive through the entire Ohio River Valley and count on two hands the number of companies using it. The story played out the same as I traveled further west into Illinois; maybe one percent of companies used liquid colorant.

Our Rosemar products sat on the early part of the new product adoption curve. In many cases, plastic products companies didn't even know they had the option of using liquid colorant. If they did know, they had an "if it ain't broke, don't fix it" attitude about the notion of switching processes.

The key was showing them the financial benefits. My basic math told me our liquid colorant helped plastics processors experience less machine downtime and operate more efficiently. Those types of incremental improvements were the only way processors could survive the intense competition coming from Asia. These companies *needed* liquid colorant; they just didn't know it. As I walked into each customer facility, I showed them how they could save time, money, and unsafe work practices on *every specialized product line* they ran. Sometimes this included dozens of lines at facilities across the country.

As floor supervisors, colorists, purchasing people, and executives watched, I did my demo, over and over again. I turned a switch on a machine that was at eye level and then stood there while colored plastic flowed into an extrusion press or injection molder.

As I did this, I thought, *No company in China is using liquid colorant. This takes a fraction of the time it takes workers in China to use solid concentrate color.*

CHAPTER 3

Makeshift Lab

JOHN

$$\left[-O - \underset{\underset{H}{|}}{\overset{\overset{CH_3}{|}}{C}} - \overset{O}{\overset{\|}{C}} - O - \right]_n$$

We started Rosemar of Ohio amid an enduring, colorful plastic boom. By the 1960s, as the material began to be used everywhere—for packaged food, consumer products, industrial products, home construction and siding, and more—American consumers went all-in. Bright, distinctive colors became big business; drab hues were out. Even vinyl siding manufacturers began using popular colors so people could custom-color their house exteriors, creating a multibillion-dollar industry.

In 1967, a group of European and American firms formed the International Colour Association, a group that helped companies such as Braun, Whirlpool, and DuPont project what colors they should add to their coffee makers, dishwashers, or carpet. Product design teams incorporated the color forecasts into their products, and the creation of a color value chain became partly responsible for shooting the country like a cannonball into the phenomenon known as "color phases."

For example, the 1970s were known as the harvest-gold and avocado-green decade, while the 1980s witnessed a mauve-and-gray period.

As colorant sellers, Mike and I knew we had to be in the field observing color first-hand and how our customers saw and reacted to it.

"We need to put miles on our cars," Mike said. "We can't sit in a lab hypothesizing all day."

Meeting with customers took money, which we lacked in our early days. Fortunately, we had grown up watching our parents work hard, so we knew what it was like to have a strong work ethic. Being a farm boy, I understood the vagaries of nature, which were often greater than the vagaries of the markets, so I wasn't overly stressed.

Mike and I made the big capital investment of purchasing an injection molding machine. In injection molding, molten plastic is squirted into a mold in the shape of the product you're trying to make, and then the mold is cooled until the product hardens. We tested liquid colorant in this process, over and over. We also bought an extrusion line. In extrusion, the machine melts the plastic as it squeezes through a die to create a certain profile. The process is much the same as using a pasta machine to make macaroni.

With these two lines, we recreated our customers' processes and invited technicians, operations people, and managers to our Rosemar of Ohio facility at the southern shore of Lake Erie to show them how our liquid colorant performed better than the solid color concentrate they used.

With no money to pay our own salaries, we hired experienced colorists, usually chemists. They worked in a makeshift lab—a claustrophobic, windowless garage in a rundown part of Cleveland—helping us develop deeper color-chemistry expertise.

Keep in mind this was before "garage entrepreneurship" was popular. There was nothing cool or retro about our garage. It was a piece of junk and no one liked working there—it was no pristine corner office or shiny new facility—and we paid no benefits, but we did our best. Our lab chemists played around with different resins and color combinations and worked with a handful of additives that could help customers get more bang for the buck from their plastics.

CHAPTER 4

What's Terracotta?

JOHN

Early on, most of our Rosemar of Ohio customers—almost all of which were from the Ohio River Valley—had simple color needs: black for trash barrels, or orange, gray, green, blue, and of course white for pipes. But others came to us with more challenging requirements. One customer I visited made a plastic flowerpot.

"This needs to look like real terracotta," he said.

I acted like I knew what "terracotta" was and thankfully figured it out when he walked over to show me a brownish-orange flowerpot.

"No problem," I lied, and went back to our lab to try to get the color just right.

We had to go through a dismaying number of iterations to achieve genuine terracotta color, which was a real time-sink. Another early customer was trying to injection mold a red purse in the shape of a strawberry for a doll that was similar to Strawberry Shortcake. When the purse came out of the press, it wasn't red at all.

"It looks red in the can, but not here," I said to the Chicago partners we worked with to match colors.

I had no idea what was going wrong, which made me uncomfortable. After making some phone calls and working in our lab, I figured out that the pigment our lab chemist had selected was heat stable to 425 degrees, but our customer was molding at 450-475 degrees, which was burning out the color.

But in addition to these chemistry and production challenges, we enjoyed some business wins. Mike's mentor and one of our first customers, Arnold Coldiron, led an effort that resulted in the trademarking of a color. He wanted the electrical switch and outlet boxes that his company, Carlon, made for housing contractors to be blue.

Arnold had us formulate the blue for him, and the blue outlet box products sold well. Within a few years, contractors in the construction industry came to identify the blue switch and outlet boxes with Carlon, so the company trademarked the name of the color, "Zip Box Blue." Later, when the US Supreme Court deemed that color could be trademarked, the company trademarked its specific hue of blue. Carlon has sold more than 150 million of those blue zip boxes over the years.

As we visited and worked with customers in those early days, we developed color expertise. We understood the process for putting color into polymers by understanding the processing industries (extrusion and injection molding), plus polymer chemistry and color chemistry. Investing in our knowledge base by buying processing equipment, hiring technicians, creating lab space, foregoing salaries, and driving all over creation in crappy cars were financial hardships, but they generated exactly the right results.

Because liquid colorant was a new category, our product was different in the marketplace. It also came "packaged" with great expertise. Our expertise helped beleaguered US plastics companies compete in a newly global economy. We didn't just sell liquid colorant; we sold improved efficiency, safety, and branding all in one pint-sized bucket.

CHAPTER 5

Opportunity Seekers

JOHN

$$\left[O - \overset{\overset{\displaystyle CH_3}{|}}{\underset{\underset{\displaystyle H}{|}}{C}} - \overset{\displaystyle O}{\overset{\|}{C}} \right]_n$$

Over time, Mike and I decided we needed to infuse more art into our selling and production processes.

"I don't really care about harvest gold and avocado green," I said, "but we do need our colorant to be exactly the same every single time we provide it to a customer."

If a customer found our colorant was dispensing inconsistently, they would have to shut down their manufacturing line or throw out a batch of product.

"Bad chemistry on our part will never be a reason for anyone throwing out our product," I promised, but I knew consistent chemistry was nothing special at all—it was the price of entry.

How we created consistency made our product different. Our few liquid colorant competitors made consistent colors with a one-size-fits-all mentality. They used the same vehicle (the liquid in which the color is dispersed) for every colorant because their big idea was to be "universally applicable." This helped make their liquid colorant consistent.

We were different.

We believed that as plastic resin formulas become more specialized and technical, the universal applicability idea—using the same vehicle for all colorants—could become a drawback.

"Being universally applicable doesn't get us the technical precision and color customization we need," one of our technicians said.

I knew we were on the right track after spending time with customers in plastics processing facilities. They told me they wanted us to make our liquid colorants *polymer-specific*, not universally applicable. If we did this, our product would be technically superior to that of our competitors.

The processors also told us they didn't want a universally applicable liquid that tried to meet everyone's needs, because consumers were demanding plastics with specific capabilities. For microwaving food, they needed polyethylene terephthalate, better known as PET; for keeping stains off their carpets, they needed nylon; for clothing with less shine, polyester; for weatherproof capabilities, PVC; and the list goes on.

As we were always prone to do, we listened to our customers. Our decision from early on to customize our liquid vehicle was different, and we were among the first liquid colorant companies to do so.

When a customer ordered red for a pipe, a doll's purse, or anything else, they received their color in the vehicle customized for their resin's composition and purpose. They received the same shade of red with no detectable difference in hue every time they ordered it. They also received their color as part of a complete system designed for them: colorant, vehicle, additives, dispensing system, and technical support.

I drove all over the Ohio River Valley, tallying new customers for our plastic colorant solutions each week. Mike and I became known as the go-to people for this new thing called liquid colorants.

"We weren't innovators so much as opportunity-seekers," I tell students and entrepreneurs who want to know how we grew our company without using outside capital.

We made chemistry, polymer science, process expertise, consistent production, and extreme customer service the combination for our success. We didn't invent the wheel. Our product was a better version of something that already existed.

CHAPTER 6

SALES FIRST!

JOHN

L uckily, Mike and I agreed on almost every aspect of how we wanted to grow our business, including financially. That alignment came in handy during more trying times, such as when Mike and I tried to get a $250,000 loan so Rosemar of Ohio could buy lab- and sample-making equipment.

It'll be no problem to get a bank loan, we had thought.

"Rosemar's inventory and receivables will be the collateral," I told Mike, "and our Chemiplast income will be the income support we need for the loan."

"No," came the response from the first loan officer—and then several others after that.

The common response went something like this: "Your Chemiplast commission income is unpredictable and unrelated to the loan, so it can't serve as the income support for the loan."

"John, we're going to need to sign the loan personally," Mike said.

This meant the banks could come after our personal assets,

including our homes, if we failed to repay the loan. We were disillusioned by this. We had never wanted to commit our homes and family savings as collateral.

"I'll ask Ray Rossman," Mike said. Ray was a bank president with whom Mike golfed.

"Great idea. He'll give us better terms," I said, still naïve. Mike knew Ray pretty well, and the guy was president of the bank. Surely, he could direct his loan officers to make concessions for us.

Ray looked at our cash forecast.

"We can loan you $50,000," he said. This was one-fifth of the amount we needed. And then he added the *coup de grace*: "You'll need to sign for this loan *personally*." I remember his words, because the "personally" was what I had hoped to avoid.

Since bank loans weren't the dream scenario we envisioned, we knew creativity was going to be key to growth. We weren't high-tech enough for venture capital investors, nor did we even want venture capital money. Instead, we'd have to raise cash the old-fashioned way—by selling our products to customers who wanted to buy them.

I thought we needed some name for this way of raising money for our business, a name that had the same cachet as "venture capital" and "working capital," and didn't sound as desperate as "bootstrapping."

I came up with the idea of SALES FIRST! We needed to get money from customers quickly, which meant we had to sell constantly and at the right time. Why not call this method SALES FIRST? I know it's not genius, but we weren't sensitive or progressive enough to have written core values for our company, nor were we smart enough to have a formal strategy. We just needed cash, and SALES FIRST! seemed like as good—or better—a strategy as any.

SALES FIRST! is a bit more nuanced than I gave it credit for, though, because it required us to consciously manage the thin line between being at the leading and the bleeding edge of the market. If we tried to open markets for liquid colorant systems too early, the sales cycle for each customer would be so long that we would have to raise capital to support our pioneering efforts. If we were too late to a market, we would face a handful of competitors who were jockeying only on price, which would erode our profits.

To survive, we learned how to do whatever it took to solve a customer need that was real, immediate, and offered a rapid payback.

CHAPTER 7

Long Live SALES FIRST!

JOHN

$$\left[-O - \underset{\underset{H}{|}}{\overset{\overset{CH_3}{|}}{C}} - \overset{\overset{O}{||}}{O} - \right]_n$$

O ur SALES FIRST! approach was vital because it allowed us to have more control over our destiny. It also kept us from trying to do something so innovative and speculative that a customer wouldn't pay for it. We let the customer lead, tell us what they wanted, and pay for it. We then delivered it with a sense of urgency. Our customers helped us stay on the leading-edge opportunity and avoid its bleeding edge.

For a long time, SALES FIRST! served as our one-and-only core value—the single most important point in how we survived and grew. Most entrepreneurs need investors for one of two reasons: their product doesn't work yet (a new medicine, for example) and needs further development, or their product requires massive infrastructure, so sales from one customer can't possibly finance all of it (for example, a railroad).

Neither of those situations applied to us. Liquid colorant was not a new medicine or railroad. It was a new category of an existing product, so it was unfamiliar but not break-through science or a massive infrastructure project.

"Our biggest barrier is that we're swimming upstream," Mike said when we put together our early sales forecasts. "We have perception issues, but we can fix those with good selling techniques."

People considered liquid color dirty, messy, and hard to implement. For every 100 doors we knocked on, 95 of the people who answered told us to pound salt. Of the remaining five, four gave excuses about why it wouldn't work for them. Liquid colorant also required a technical sale. I met first with process engineers, bench chemists, foremen, and production managers on the factory floor, which was where I felt most at home. I showed them how our product helped them reduce machine downtime and increase productivity.

They liked this and asked the company's purchasing department to figure the cost of liquid colorant.

"Too expensive," purchasing almost always responded.

Raw materials, not labor, were the largest cost component of extruded and injection-molded plastic products. Resin was roughly 80 percent of the raw materials cost, and additives, about 20 percent. Purchasers were always looking for ways to reduce materials costs.

I was an avid back-of-the-envelope number cruncher, so I loved to combat this objection with a couple of calculations.

"Okay, you're processing 10 million pounds of resin per month and using a letdown ratio (LDR) of 2 percent pellet concentrate," I explained. "That's 20,000 pounds per month of concentrate at $1.50 per pound, or $30,000. Our liquid concentrate sells for $2.10 per pound, but you only use it at 1.2 percent LDR. Since you only have to purchase 12,000 pounds per month of colorant, the cost is $25,200, or $4,800 per month in savings. Annually, you'll save more than

$57,000—plus the additional savings of decreased warehousing space."

Great execution of SALES FIRST! required driving everywhere and showing people these back-of-the-envelope calculations.

With SALES FIRST!, Mike and I also made sure not to overestimate the revenue or profit we could generate. "I don't wanna be one of those entrepreneurs who fails because we sat in our offices *thinking* about what we can do or how fast we can do it," I said to Mike.

We knew from our previous sales experience that revenue usually came in slower than expected. The office dwellers failed more often because they weren't out in the field being told "no" over and over again, gaining an understanding of what real-world (not hypothesized!) patterns united the "yeses."

SALES FIRST! united Mike and me, but it sometimes frustrated employees. When employees asked if they could spend money on something, Mike and I habitually made a motion of opening our wallets and doling out dollar bills. We wanted to show that our culture rested on the fact that we were financing every spending decision ourselves. We didn't have money to take on speculative or long-payoff projects. Our SALES FIRST! culture relied on near-term opportunities that we could financially justify.

Because of SALES FIRST! we often rebuffed employees who had exciting growth opportunities they wanted to pursue. Although frustrating to others, this approach enabled Mike and me to avoid bankruptcy, slowly build our company, and avoid having to answer to equity holders, creditors, a board of directors, or other investors. With SALES

FIRST! we didn't need to ask anyone else for an opinion about whether we could deliver when a customer needed something.

We trusted each other to make the right SALES FIRST! decisions for the company and the customer.

CHAPTER 8

Learning to Sell

MIKE

In some ways, both John and I had been preparing for the SALES FIRST! strategy for our entire careers. Before we were scrappy plastics guys who didn't want to (and couldn't) take on venture capital—or any other capital, for that matter—driving around the Ohio River Valley trying to sell people our wares, we were soaking up sales knowledge from our bosses and mentors at our first post-college jobs.

In 1965, I graduated from St. Louis University, a Jesuit school where I majored in chemistry and minored in math. After college, I started in a sales support position at Mallinckrodt Chemical, which manufactured chemicals products ranging from turf grass fungicides to paper mill chemicals and plastics additives. Eventually, my skills developed enough that I began visiting customers myself and was put in charge of my own territory, eastern Ohio to western New York and West Virginia.

Just before I turned 30, I found a new job at a different company, Cincinnati Milacron, which had a chemicals business that produced chemical additives for plastics processors.

In selling these additives to the plastics processors, I also could use my chemistry background.

I took over the company's Cleveland, Ohio, territory, and spent my days selling heat stabilizer for use in polyvinyl chloride applications. PVC is used mostly in plastic pipes and vinyl house siding. When it's heated, its chemical properties change, and the heat stabilizer I sold remediated these changes.

My boss was Howard Ellerhorst, Jr., a gregarious and polished man who became a mentor and showed me the sales ropes. Howard took me with him to meetings with executives at major industrial names in the Cleveland area and showed me how to conduct myself once I was there.

"Most importantly," he said, a commandment that I well remember, "Do not *ever* waste your customer's time."

When I started hopping in my green Ford Torino and driving around Ohio, Howard sometimes came along for the ride, but mostly I was on my own. In both cases, I enjoyed good success and was happy.

Within a year, Howard made me sales manager for the entire Midwest region. I had a lot of responsibility for a 30-year-old but woke up each day ready to practice everything I had learned about selling over the prior eight years.

Unfortunately, Howard decided to retire and start his own consulting business, and I had a new boss who was ineffective, couldn't sell, and was a crummy manager.

This was the first major disappointment in my career—the first time I didn't wake up every day loving sales.

CHAPTER 9

Sales Rep

MIKE

Even though I was disappointed with my boss at Cincinnati Milacron, I was always hungry to learn more and worked to stay on the cutting-edge of industry trends. I started building relationships with downstream plastics processors, whereas most chemical salespeople were calling on upstream resin compounders. I knew that the plastics processers were deciding to cut out the compounders and mix the chemicals themselves, right on their own factory floor, before making pipe or vinyl siding. I also steered Cincinnati Milacron's salesforce in this direction.

My prescience about the industry direction and my relationships with plastics processers would prove to be very useful to a company named Synpro and its owner, Gary Curtiss. A family business, Synpro produced and sold additives to the PVC industry for use in plastic pipe. It had recently been acquired by a much larger company, Dart & Kraft, but Gary was running Synpro as an independent division.

During a lunch, Gary told me that Synpro's business

was changing. So many plastics processors were mixing resin themselves and no longer buying from the chemical compounders—just as I had predicted—that Synpro's traditional business of selling into the compounder market was evaporating. He needed direct relationships with the plastics extruders.

I thought he wanted me to work on staff for him—but Gary had other ideas.

"What if I make you your own man as an independent sales rep?" he asked.

In other words, I would leave Cincinnati Milacron and start representing Synpro's chemical additives to plastics extrusion companies.

Sales repping was common in the chemical additives industry because it was more cost-efficient for the largely mom-and-pop chemical additives companies to promote their products via independent sales agents. There was also big money in the commissions that reps received from principals like Synpro.

I told him my dilemma: I lived paycheck-to-paycheck and didn't have savings to sustain me while I built up my book of business.

Gary wasn't fazed and asked, "What would it take, money-wise, for you to live for six months?"

I told him that, and my potential travel costs.

"Okay, I'll give you that amount every month, and when your commissions reach a sustainable level, you can pay me back."

His easy confidence in my abilities surprised me. I think, professionally, someone who has more confidence in you than you have in yourself is a mentor.

I also confessed I had no idea if any of my current Cincinnati Milacron customers would actually buy Synpro additives from me.

However, Gary knew Synpro had a highly respected product line and encouraged me to call and ask them. I mulled over this offer as I went back to work.

CHAPTER 10

Angel Customers

MIKE

I first called Arnold Coldiron, vice president of manufacturing at Carlon, which made Hula Hoops but was also
one of the largest plastic pipe manufacturers on the planet,
churning out 200 million pounds of pipe per year. I told him
I was thinking of leaving Cincinnati Milacron to become an
independent sales rep.

After he told me he was surprised I didn't make this move
earlier, I got straight to the point.

"I have a little problem, in terms of capital. To start my
own thing, I'm going to need help. Would you be willing to
place your business with me?"

I wasn't asking him to move his business away from Cincinnati Milacron. Ten or more additives go into PVC—
thermal stabilizers, lubricants, fillers, processing aids—so I
was asking him to become a customer of a Synpro additive
that Cincinnati Milacron didn't sell.

"Look," he said, "I buy products from a lot of people,
and as long as you have a competitive price and the quality
is there, then I would love to buy from you. You're a person

who always brings me something interesting to discuss. You don't waste my time."

"I don't see this as me doing you a favor," he said later in our conversation, "because I have a selfish rationale. I have no interest in building new relationships with new salespeople."

Newly confident, I called up several other customers and secured commitments from them as well. But among the handful of calls I made, I counted the one to Arnold as the most important. He committed right away, and in a big way, to my idea of striking out on my own, becoming the "angel customer" and boost I needed to go out on my own. He put me into the repping business.

I left Cincinnati Milacron, and on May 1, 1978, Gary Curtiss wrote a check for my salary and business expense advances. I was officially an independent rep, exclusively selling Synpro products.

CHAPTER 11

A Pretty Riotous Guy

MIKE

Then, Gary called me one day to ask me to take on more business.

"Gary, I can handle only a certain number of customers at one time," I said. "I'm working all the time just to keep up with the amount of business I have."

But you could not successfully say "no" to Gary. He always had a solution.

"What about John?" he asked.

Gary's idea was sound. John Haugh was a salesman at Cincinnati Milacron I had hired away from General Mills because he was plain-spoken, purposeful, had big goals, and had an undergraduate chemistry degree. At Cincinnati Milacron, we had covered sales territories together and become friends. We often had two-martini lunches, spending our noon hour at dive bars revisiting what we had sold that day and strategizing on what we wanted to sell the next day.

John was a pretty riotous guy, one of those types who can spontaneously tell jokes that, at a minimum, get a chuckle and usually a big laugh. He was totally immature and about

17 years old in much of his thinking. More than once, I watched him take a glass of ouzo, a Greek liqueur, and drink it without using his hands.

I also knew that John liked and respected me.

"I'm going to be as good as you one day," he had once said to me after I had won a big account for Cincinnati Milacron.

"What makes you think you're not already?" I had asked. I thought he worked hard and had deep product knowledge and effective selling skills. "You've already got my selling capability in spades."

I called up John, and while he was surprised when I asked him to explore the independent rep business, I steadily reeled him in.

"I can't think of a good reason why not," John eventually said. "I get along great with Gary. He wouldn't holler at a cat if it peed on the couch." John knew Gary would be as good a principal as a rep could find. He had a relentless belief in people he liked, and he matched it with disarming niceness.

"And I think you and I get along well, too," John added.

In April 1979, a year after I left Cincinnati Milacron to be an independent sales rep, John Haugh agreed to join me as a partner. He added his long list of potential plastics processing company relationships to mine, which gave us a healthy stable of new prospects. We sold them Synpro's heat stabilizers and lubricants.

Selling these top products and bringing our chemistry backgrounds and market knowledge to each sales call, we became really credible! We also were, we thought, pretty cool—sporting 1970s sideburns and bell-bottom pants. We loved becoming known as suave polymer-industry experts. Chemiplast was on its way!

CHAPTER 12

Walking a Tightrope

MIKE

Things with Chemiplast were going smoothly—until Gary Curtiss, our only principal at Synpro, left. We weren't surprised by his departure, as the CEO of an acquired company often leaves his new position, and Synpro had recently become the plastic additives division of Dart & Kraft. But with Gary gone, Dart & Kraft's management told us they wanted to build an in-house sales team and terminated our agreement. We found ourselves with virtually no income.

Although we were scrappy, the near future was rough. Through John's contact at a Japanese firm, we picked up a new principal to rep, the PVC resin producer Shintech. After a few years, our Shintech contact said, essentially, that they could pay the customers we had brought to them directly—and Chemiplast was out of a gig and a revenue stream.

Next, we connected with the Texas-based Hitox—which had a beige titanium dioxide pigment product that was useful for creating opacity and improving tint strength—and helped it get into the PVC pipe industry. Since we had "ins" with makers of pipes that were green, purple, blue, and black, and we figured out a way for Hitox to include its beige pigment in those pipes. The new business we landed for them ended up filling 60 percent of their plant.

After two or three years, Hitox too terminated their sales repping agreement with us. Chemiplast had no revenue coming in the door yet again.

"John, we've got to manage our relationships with these guys so we make enough money to support ourselves but not so much that they want to fire us," I said.

"Yeah, it's like walking a tightrope," John said. "It's not much fun. If we're successful, we're fired—and if we're unsuccessful, we'll be fired."

Of course, it wasn't just our livelihoods at stake. The repping business we did with Chemiplast served as the ATM for our fledgling liquid colorant business Rosemar of Ohio—and the latter depended on this revenue stream for survival.

CHAPTER 13

Things Fall Apart

MIKE

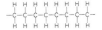

The limitations of our business model became even clearer when another important relationship fell apart.

A couple of years into our partnership with the Rosemar liquid colorants team in Chicago, we found that they were responding less and less to our technical needs. In fact, our partnership began to slowly go downhill. Knowing we couldn't turn back and reverse the partnership, I decided we needed to invest in it.

Unfortunately, they were *divesting* from it, which I discovered when we were sharing a booth with them at a national plastics exposition in Chicago.

"Listen," the grayest-haired of the three partners said to me, "we have a deal to sell our company to Morton-Thiokol."

He had intimated previously that he needed to think about his future and retirement; he frequently talked about his 84-year-old aunt who was an investor in the company and interested in cashing out. Meanwhile, Morton-Thiokol was a Midwestern company with $2 billion in revenue. It thought Rosemar could help it renew its polymer innovation capabilities.

"Is the deal to sell Rosemar of Ohio, too?" I asked him.

"The whole thing," he said.

Our partners owned Rosemar Industries entirely, but they owned only 49 percent of Rosemar Industries of Ohio. Only John and I had the right to sell our share. I watched smiling convention attendees sauntering by our booth and wished I had their peace of mind. I was growing concerned.

"How much do we get for it?" I asked.

"You and John each get $250,000."

That's a lot of money, I thought, and then a second later, I felt insulted: *They didn't have the right to sell Rosemar of Ohio.* A second later, I was elated again: *This is the big time!*

My emotions fluctuated because we needed the money. In 2020 dollars, $250,000 is more than $650,000.

CHAPTER 14

Lack of Goodwill

MIKE

A s I tried to figure out whether I was happy or annoyed, one of the partners outlined the rest of the deal. He said the three of them would get $4 million to split among them, and they would have management jobs with Morton-Thiokol.

"How about us? Do we have jobs?" I asked.

"No, unfortunately they have concerns about you," he said and explained that one of the principals we repped at Chemiplast was a competitor to Morton-Thiokol. "Because of that, the Morton-Thiokol executive team doesn't want you coming on board."

Apparently, as a condition of sale, Morton-Thiokol would require us to sign a non-compete agreement that applied not only to Rosemar of Ohio but also to Mike's and my Chemiplast business.

My evolving reaction was that this wasn't a good deal for us. Before I left our convention booth to do homework on the deal, I felt pretty sure I wanted to turn it down. From the warning John issued them, I could tell he felt the same way.

"Remember," he said. "We own the majority of Rosemar of Ohio."

As soon as we walked out of earshot of the partners, I said, "They can't sell without us. You and I need to approve. Let's figure this out."

I read Rosemar of Ohio's buy-sell agreement and confirmed we were right—they could sell our company only with our permission.

Knowing that we wouldn't have jobs with Morton-Thiokol and would also be prohibited from making a living because of the non-compete, we decided $250,000 for each of us wasn't enough money.

The next day, we sat down with the partners in Chicago. As our strategist, I started the conversation. I explained that they needed to tell the acquisition team at Morton-Thiokol that we needed more money for us to agree to be out of jobs and live under the other restrictive terms of the proposed agreement. With some annoyance and no contrition, our Chicago partners explained that they hadn't told Morton-Thiokol they lacked control of Rosemar of Ohio.

"Well, that's unfortunate," I said. "I guess you'll have to go back and explain that fact to them."

Their lack of goodwill shocked me. John and I believed partners should never self-deal, hide things, or negotiate for one member of the partnership and not the other.

Under duress, our Chicago partners went back to Morton-Thiokol.

"It's not enough money," they apparently said to the executives there, or something like that. I wasn't in the room but was later told that the conversation didn't go well. The multibillion-dollar company apparently was unwilling to pay a dime more for our portion of the business and quickly called off the deal.

More damage was done by this foiled transaction than lost time and focus. Our trust with our partners dissolved. We then knew that not only had they stopped supporting our technical needs but also they were prepared to ink deals that weren't in our best interest. They saw us as being prepared to hold them back from the financial future they needed as they approached retirement. Furious and disappointed, we stopped speaking with them, and vice versa.

CHAPTER 15

The FBI Raid

MIKE

Then, the FBI raided our Rosemar of Ohio facility. On a Friday night while I was changing into a tuxedo for a benefit dinner, I received a call from a federal authority. Initially, I thought, *This is a practical joke.*

"We're conducting a search of your plant," the agent on the phone said and then told me I had exactly one hour to get to our Rosemar of Ohio plant in downtown Cleveland before they'd break down the door.

This wasn't a practical joke! I called John.

"Do you know what's going on, John?"

"No, I have no idea at all. Why do they want to break down the door?" he asked, "We have keys."

Whatever was going on, breaking down the door seemed to both of us to be melodramatic and unnecessary. I drove to the plant where two federal authorities and our lab technician awaited us. We opened the door for them, and they walked in. The lab technician showed them where our file cabinets were located.

"What's going on?" I asked an authority.

He said, "We're seeking data to support an accusation by an employee regarding your company's use of a chemical in an application that may be dangerous to consumers."

This suspicion likely stemmed from the general legal environment surrounding chemicals companies at the time. Months earlier, the owner of an unrelated Midwestern company had been sent to prison for life for manufacturing chemicals he knew to be dangerous. As a result, lawyers were seeking to take on cases by employees against manufacturing firm owners everywhere. Our employee accuser had heard (incorrectly) that our business was possibly up for sale, decided it was because we were trying to avoid liability (it wasn't), and found a sympathetic ear in the FBI.

Now, it just so happened that this employee also was going through a very difficult time in his private family life. Fearing that his job might disappear added to his stress and belief in the world being against him. He went from being a seemingly happy employee to developing outright animosity and paranoia about us. Convinced that he had a case against us, he went to the authorities.

This caused us a year of indescribable angst.

"The authorities are treating us as if we're guilty until proven innocent," I said to our lawyer, Tom Jones.

The wheels of justice grind slowly, and for six or eight months, we tried to run the business while the investigation took place. On Tom's advice, we immediately disclosed to our customers what was going on, even though we were in the dark about most of it. I was never sure we wouldn't go to jail because anti-corporate, anti-chemical company sentiment pervaded America. The authorities prevented us from talking to them or our employees about any specifics of the investigation. They told us only Tom, our lawyer, could talk with anyone about anything related to the charges, and even then, only when the authorities said he could.

We were powerless and completely in the dark.

I slept very little, and neither John nor I could eat much. We lost weight. Our friends told us we looked run-down and ill.

Eight months of us being unable to sell product turned into a year. And then one day, just like that, the FBI cleared us of any wrongdoing. They found out what we knew all along and what we had tried to tell them on the rare occasions they asked us for information: The accusations by our employee were completely baseless. The authorities found nothing to support the employee's baseless claims and would not charge us with a crime.

We were incredibly relieved and angry all at once—angry because we should not have been put in a position of feeling elated about not going to jail for something we didn't do, something that was based on one employee's instability and a situation in which a team of federal agents found not one single fact supporting the accuser's claim.

"This experience will never leave me," I said to John.

John agreed. "It's hard not to be bitter."

But, then again, throughout this ordeal, our relationships with customers grew stronger than ever because we informed them of what was going on to the extent we were able. They valued our forthrightness in the face of inconceivable uncertainty about what was going to happen to us and our business.

In contrast, our Chicago partners believed and supported the claims made by the rogue employee and only talked to us through lawyers. Their standoffishness didn't improve after investigators found the employee's accusation to be baseless. Not one of our Chicago partners called us—until they had a proposal.

"We'll never reconcile our differences," one of the partners said. "Why don't you and John buy out our 49 percent of Rosemar of Ohio?"

He was right; we needed to end our partnership. We scrounged up $185,000 to purchase their ownership of Rosemar of Ohio. They received a cash infusion from us and benefited from a separate deal by negotiating an acquisition of their company by Ferro Corporation, a large Cleveland-based specialty-chemicals concern. At the tail ends of their careers, they needed retirement money, and they got it. They were happy.

John and I were in the early days of our careers and investing for our future. We had gone through an investigation by federal authorities and what felt to us like a traitorous relationship with our partners. Needing a fresh start, we changed the name of our company from Rosemar Industries of Ohio to ColorMatrix Corporation.

We closed out our past and gave ourselves, we hoped, a bright future.

CHAPTER 16

Our 50-50 Partnership

MIKE

Over the prior couple of years, John and I had experienced a series of disappointments that had been real blows to us.

I had left my first post-college job at Mallinckrodt Chemical for Cincinnati Milacron, where the successor to Howard Ellerhorst, my beloved boss and mentor, didn't care about me.

I had left that job to become an independent sales rep for Synpro and teamed up with John, but our relationship with Synpro ended when Gary Curtiss left.

After that, John's and my relationships with every principal we repped through our business Chemiplast had ended, which threatened to disrupt the cashflow to our burgeoning liquid colorant business, Rosemar of Ohio.

Then our relationship with one of our technical employees had devolved into a false accusation of fraud. And our relationship with our three Chicago partners in Rosemar Industries had been obliterated.

Although many mentors had helped us tremendously

along the way, the disappointments also had shattered our idealism. Being fired, duped, and wrongly accused, we had become cynics.

Yet these disappointments made the bond John and I shared even more solid. We had a relationship of mutual respect—one that honored our differences instead of trying to paper over them. Our partnership was one of our company's greatest assets, seeing us through the major disappointments that transpire in business.

He and I had even set up the part of Rosemar Industries of Ohio that we owned as a fifty-fifty partnership.

"You know this is risky," our lawyer had told us at the time.

He had explained that equal co-ownership is a risky business structure that frequently fails.

"Your equal-partners approach requires relationship skills as much as it requires specific legal documents," he said. "One of you contributes more than the other and becomes disgruntled. Then you're in a logjam situation because neither of you has the right of majority ownership." He continued, trying to dissuade us from using our preferred structure. "With three equal partners, two can make decisions to overrule the third, but not so with two."

"But there are occasions when a fifty-fifty partnership can work," I countered.

"The thing that's frustrating is that so many of the people we've been good to have turned on us," John said once over drinks. "And yet we're still stupid enough to believe our partnership with each other is going to succeed. Why is that?"

I told him that I thought the reason was we focused on differentiation through our roles and personalities. As it turned out, we felt time and time again, that for us, this was the right way to go. Whenever we would encounter a steady drumbeat of difficulty over the coming decades, we would turn to each other for help.

CHAPTER 17

Like Brothers

MIKE

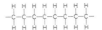

John and I loved each other like brothers and respected each other's differences, an amazing combination that gave us our best chance at success with our company. We also focused on our roles and responsibilities. I was CEO and John was president. In my role, I led our vision, strategy, and technology decisions. Data-driven to the core, I continuously asked people to provide me with data and facts so John and I could make objective decisions.

"Don't give me things you call facts if they aren't really facts," I frequently told people.

I looked at markets and customer accounts objectively and built up a point of view on how to grow our business. I loved to place big, strategic decisions in front of people, listen to their thoughts, and then work with John to decide.

Doing this, I sometimes came across as impatient and arrogant.

"Mike, if you're dealing with actual facts and your counterpart is basing their decision on opinion or hope disguised as a fact, you start to tune them out," John said to me once after a meeting.

"You think I did that?" I asked him.

"Yeah, you did it, and you do it a lot. It doesn't bother me, but it bothers others."

We felt optimistic about our equal partnership, though, believing our strong relationship would overcome our inevitable disagreements.

"You know, liking each other is not just a soft-fuzzy feeling. It's a matter of our company's success," John said.

He was right. We *had* to like each other. Fortunately, I liked John. He was very funny, a little wild, and an adrenaline junkie. Over the course of our long partnership, he got into racing Cigarette-type boats on Lake Erie, shooting skeet at competitive levels, and racing cars around the country. His skeet shooting pastime was amusing to me because it drew a crowd of regular guys who could barely afford shells, as well as billionaires who loved the sport for its aristocratic British heritage (it helped refine bird hunting skills). He also was consumed with cleanliness. When in doubt, he cleaned. I often went into the office to find him cleaning his desk, carpet, and windows.

Often, when I asked, "Where's John?" the answer came back, "Cleaning his boat . . ." (or car, or house, or something else).

Professionally, John abhorred doing paperwork and loved operations. He was in his element on a manufacturing floor or interacting with customers to get them what they needed. His first instinct was to get in front of customers quickly and resolve their problems immediately. He gathered facts and details so he could fix a situation, and he followed this process like a bricklayer building a house, minute after minute, hour after hour, year after year, diligently and speedily gathering facts, getting in front of customers, and solving their problems.

He was no speech maker. His words were the opposite of fancy.

"I'm as blunt as a two-by-four," he said about himself, which was true.

However, he was so unassuming and motivated to succeed that his bluntness was endearing.

"Almost everyone finds him easy to relate to," I said to my wife once. "He builds great relationships with customers."

Our customers saw integrity in his quickness to speak the truth with no veil or preamble.

"Initially, they're taken aback, but they come to appreciate his directness. You have to see it to believe it."

But probably the most interesting thing about John was, in the midst of the adrenaline sports, tough talk, and quick problem solving, he was a *total* softie. Part of his soft-heartedness was purposeful. His professional MO was to overlook people's flaws.

"I don't want to be like a big-company bureaucrat spending all my days trying to help the people on my team try to improve on their weaknesses, because then I would just have a team of people with watered-down skill sets," he said.

"I think it's far more productive to spend my time building up people's strengths. If they can sell like a maniac or put together a great financial statement, I'm happy to ignore their flaws."

The part of John's soft-heartedness that was not purposeful or strategic—but just his nature—is harder to describe, but I'll try. He was intuitive, and when a person came to know him, they'd hit that layer of intuition like a well driller hitting water. At first, they saw a gruff joke teller who was all about getting things done for customers, and then they might be sitting around a conference table one day when he showed a completely unexpected sensitivity, emotion, or depth about an employee, friend, or politician. I sometimes found this soft layer to be problematic—he empathized with people's difficulties so much that our workers knew to go straight to John with their issues.

"You know, John, the word on the floor is that people will get the answer they want from you," I said to him.

He admitted that he knew this to be true, but we agreed there wasn't a lot we could or would do about it. It's hard to change human nature.

CHAPTER 18

Making Decisions

MIKE

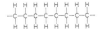

Considering that there was constant risk in what we were doing—liquid colorants were new in the industry and untested in most applications—I took on the role of facing risks head-on and minimizing them in a consistent way. Through gathering information, we gained confidence that we were making the best decisions we could.

John and I never sat on decisions. We made them and moved forward. We didn't always agree on every decision, but we recognized there was more than one way to skin every cat. If we disagreed, we knew one of us wasn't all right and the other all wrong. We knew a black-and-white mentality like that would set us up for failure. For the sake of the survival of our partnership, we came to an understanding that we simply had to decide without recrimination. If the decider ended up, in retrospect, making the wrong decision, then so be it. We liked and respected each other enough that we worked through any problems.

"We need to always resolve our differences between ourselves rather than contradict each other in front of employees," I said to him.

"Well, I agree with that," he said, "I think our relationship is very solid, and our employees need to know that."

We felt free to challenge one another directly, and so, in addition to love and mutual respect, directness and rapid decision making became hallmarks of our relationship.

"Why did you tell (insert name) that? You should have told him this," we could say to each other without threat to our relationship.

To the point of rapid decision-making, we never created a board of directors or board of advisors.

"That'll just slow down our decision making," John said.

"I think you're right," I agreed. "What about investors? Any desire to take them on, or are you still interested in us operating on a shoestring?"

"No interest in venture capital," he replied, "And I don't think they'd have any interest in us. They'd slow us down, or they'd be like our principals, Mike. They'll fire us if we're unsuccessful, and they'd fire us if we're successful."

He was right—even if we succeeded, they'd probably want new executives who could grow our company faster than us.

"Okay, we'll keep raising money the old-fashioned way," I concluded.

The old-fashioned way of financing our company was getting customers to pay us for something of value. While the Asian tiger was rising—the Asian tiger was the huge economic force of Asia in manufacturing; a massive competitor that created a sense of urgency in our industry—and Silicon Valley was luring talent with its siren song of smart, powerful money, our old-fashioned method was to bootstrap our way to success. John and I agreed on this; our industry's growth rate allowed us to buy nice suits and cars but never reached levels that would attract meaningful venture capital money.

Our approach to business also led me to become dedicated to philanthropy in a way that I wouldn't have predicted. I would eventually realize I loved providing opportunities to people and would find some of my greatest happiness in life by helping people get out of a tough spot, believing in them, and watching them grow.

PART II

Growing

CHAPTER 19

Beers at the Holiday Inn

MIKE

SALES FIRST! came about by necessity. We were hardly strategists, consultants, innovators, or anything else. We were opportunists without a lot of connections who needed to sell.

If our business was to grow, we needed to bring in some SALES FIRST! devotees. We found our man at a trade show. John and I stood at our company booth at a plastics convention in Cleveland, talking to passers-by who showed interest in liquid colorants. A big guy—6'3" and about 250 pounds—introduced himself.

"Hi, I'm Dave McBride." He was young, early 20s, and his nametag showed that he worked for Reed Plastics, a Dallas, Texas, company that made dry color concentrates. He told us he was Reed's inside sales associate, taking and fulfilling customer orders, and his boss had recently transferred him to Ohio.

"I think liquid colorant is going to take market share from solid concentrate," he said, "and I'm excited by that. I'd love to be on the liquid colorant side." He seemed genuinely excited, an attitude we liked. He had majored in marketing at the University of Illinois and seemed smart and insightful.

"If you're ever looking for someone to sell for you," he said, "let me know."

Soon thereafter, John and I interviewed him over beers at a local Holiday Inn.

"I'm confident I can sell your liquid colorants," he said.

We chatted more, finished our beers, and left. The next day we offered him a job as our first salesperson. Our annual sales then totaled around $1 million.

"Okay, Dave," John said, "your job is to go out and sell as much of our liquid colorant as you can to plastics injection molders in the Ohio Valley." We were still, at the time, Rosemar of Ohio, and our partnership with Rosemar Industries required that we sell only in the Ohio Valley.

One day, Dave sold ten drums of white liquid colorant to a company that made components for Whirlpool washing machines. "I just got my first customer order," he said as he strolled into my office.

"That's great!" I replied. "I told you it would happen."

He acted nonchalant, but I wanted to celebrate his first sale for us. I called John into my office so we could make a big stink out of it. We finally had someone else selling for us. Seeing our excitement, Dave became more obviously happy about his success. He was a natural, and we knew he was going to work out well.

CHAPTER 20

Polyetheylene Terepthalate

MIKE

After we split from our Chicago partners, the world beyond the Ohio Valley opened up to us. Dave added new geographies. Some companies in these areas started talking about polyethylene terephthalate. Invented in 1941, PET was a strong, lightweight, 100-percent recyclable plastic. Bottlers began to use it in the 1970s. In Europe, it became the leading material for food and beverage packaging, and the US soon followed suit.

Dave McBride brought on one of the largest glass bottle manufacturers in the world as his first PET packaging customer. He was visiting the company's prescription products division in Ohio, which made amber-colored polypropylene pill vials. Dave converted them to liquid concentrate for that application, and while he was there, he noticed they had a couple of machines in another room that were making PET cough syrup bottles.

"How do you get the amber color into those cough syrup bottles?" he asked.

"We buy pre-colored resin," his contact said. He told Dave

that they were buying pre-color from the specialty chemicals divisions of a couple of large commodity suppliers.

"Buying amber pre-color this way is expensive," Dave said. He sat down and showed them the numbers. "You should buy clear resin and add our liquid color on site. It would be less expensive."

They agreed, but they told him that adding liquid colorant to PET resin affected its physical integrity. They tasked him with finding a liquid vehicle that would work in PET. This was no easy task because PET is a pretty sensitive polymer and doesn't offer the kind of technical forgiveness as polyolefins. He came back to us, explained the situation, and our technical crew engineered a solution. Thanks to the technical team's work, the company became Dave's first customer conversion in the rapidly growing PET packaging industry, and that marked another major milestone for Dave and us.

CHAPTER 21

Great Relationships

JOHN

$$\left[-O-\underset{\underset{H}{|}}{\overset{\overset{CH_3}{|}}{C}}-\overset{\overset{O}{||}}{O}-\right]_n$$

Many people think that to build great relationships, they should sweep problems under the rug and avoid confrontations. But the opposite is true. We always quickly came straight to the point and laid issues right out onto the table in front of everyone.

"What do we need to do to get this fixed?" we asked.

If we messed up and confessed, we had the possibility of repairing the relationship. If we tried to downplay issues on either side, or not tell customers about problems, we could not repair the relationship. Either we or they felt too frustrated to make the relationship worth repairing. Relationships with direct communication are important to a successful SALES FIRST! approach.

To forge great relationships, we spent as much face-to-face time with customers as possible. No customer should have had to call us with requests like, "Can you give me a quote on (such and such product)?" We needed to be close enough to them that we could anticipate their needs. We needed to be in front of our customers, listening to their problems and developing relationships with them. When we followed this path, we built a suite of customers who became the cornerstone of our business.

Our early work with Carlon's Arnold Coldiron offers one example of how our relationships with customers worked. He had become the largest customer of our Chemiplast repping business by agreeing to purchase one of Synpro's additives (calcium stearate) from us. Then we wanted him to help us out at Rosemar.

"Would Carlon be willing to replace the solid color concentrate it's using with our liquid concentrate?" I asked him.

He thought it might. His R&D team, which researched new resins, stabilizers, waxes, fillers, and colors for Carlon's switch boxes and plastic pipes, tested our liquid colorant in its Oklahoma City facility and decided it was good.

"My engineers tell me your product works," he said, "and we've got a great relationship already. So, I'm willing to work with you to switch to liquid colorant."

Our longstanding relationship led to this huge, early win.

CHAPTER 22

Liquid Carbon Black

JOHN

M y experience with Bill Coleman, general manager at
the vinyl siding company Variform, also illustrates the
importance of strong customer relationships. We originally
met him when we sold him resin and heat stabilizer additives
through Chemiplast. Then he became a manager at a vinyl
siding plant that extruded siding that was one color on the
top and gray on the bottom. He wanted to switch to our
liquid colorant for this co-extrusion, but he was concerned
that liquid colorant was messier than dry pellets. We fought
this perception every day, in general, and we lost many customer prospects because of the belief that liquid color would
cover their machines, employees, and factory floors.

I decided to bring a can of liquid carbon black (the messiest liquid colorant) on a flight to visit Bill at his Kansas
plant. I wanted him to see that even the messiest colorant
was neat. Bill knew me well enough to know that I was
obsessively clean—and that if I said something was clean, it
was immaculate.

I brought my dispensing pump with me on the plane

and wore nice slacks and a tie to impress upon Bill that our product was so clean, you could easily handle it while wearing business attire. I had made this my standard technique for preempting the customer concern about liquid colorant being messy—if a neat freak like me could handle it in a suit, then their skilled supervisors, foremen, and chemists could handle it on the factory floor.

Just before we started the demo, Bill unexpectedly stopped me.

"I'll do this," he said, indicating he wanted to operate the pump that metered the liquid colorant into the throat of the extruder.

I hadn't planned on this. "Bill, I was going to show you how to do this first," I said.

"Nah, let me do it."

He was wearing a pink shirt and gray tie and slacks. I was a little nervous as I watched him, but mostly, I was confident. He pulled off the cover of the carton of carbon black and . . . it burst! It covered him from his shoes to his nose! I mean, he was *covered* in black liquid.

"I should probably catch an earlier flight," I said sheepishly.

The flight to Kansas must have pressurized the can so that it burst when he opened it. Fortunately, Bill had a great sense of humor, and although the colorant ruined his clothes, we could use the remainder of the liquid black for the demonstration. I completed the trial successfully and secured Variform as a customer.

That disaster turned into a success only because Bill and I had a great relationship. I am pretty certain if we hadn't known and trusted each other, he would have booted me out of the facility.

Solving issues quickly also make a difference, especially when we experienced quality problems. We had an issue once with a multibillion-dollar building-products company in the South. They claimed our orange colorant was burning and discoloring as it went through the manufacturing process. Mike went to see them, and our main customer contact immediately handed him a product-liability claim for $85,000. On the spot, Mike said he'd take care of the issue, no problem.

"Enter a credit balance of $85,000 into the customer's account," Mike said to our vice president of finance.

When I later visited the customer, our speed to resolve had clearly resonated.

"Mike, this guy's boss complimented him because he resolved the problem so quickly," I told him. "And some of the bad material has value in a second-hand market, so our customer can mitigate a portion of the $85,000 that way, as well."

CHAPTER 23

Clubs, Airplanes

JOHN

Mike and I believed ColorMatrix could only be as good as its vendors. We wanted to have a suite of relationships with vendors who helped us strategically and acted as partners in growing our business.

We began interrogating the owners of businesses we admired.

"Who can't you live without?"

"Who do you rely on for your success?"

"Which lawyer is really worth their salt?"

Then, we put the recommended vendors through the gauntlet. We asked them to explain relevant experiences in detail, checked references extensively, and, most importantly, let them know we expected to build long-term relationships.

"I'm different from a big company client," I told them. "Big company executives think about the relationship as a corporate one. I want personalized service." I was looking for "*my* accountant," "*my* lawyer," "*my* banker."

"I'm anxious about *everything*," I told them. "I value accessibility. Mike and I have a sense of urgency; we're impatient. We want answers as soon as we ask questions, and we need vendors who understand this."

Mike's membership at a local country club proved to be fertile ground for us in finding the right vendors. We hired a local accounting firm who called back immediately, helped us with monthly bookkeeping, and then dragged us into the computer age. They understood our big ambitions and became partners in these ambitions. More strategically, they helped us better position ourselves with banks so we could get loans. The new accountants told us, "We'll clean up and organize your books on a consistent basis so when you go to banks, you're professionalized and come across as worthy of a loan."

At the same country club, Mike also came across Dick Musgrave, a terrific insurance agent. He not only helped us secure our entire insurance portfolio but also found us our first manufacturing facility. A non-profit board of trustees he sat on had received a donation of a 50,000-square-foot building in Midtown Cleveland. The Boys & Girls Clubs couldn't afford to maintain or operate that large of a building.

"I think you could probably have this place for nothing," Dick said to Mike. "You'd need to give the Boys & Girls Clubs some office space, but you could have the rest of it."

We ended up paying taxes, operating costs, and maintenance, but making no monthly lease payment, which was a fantastic deal. We took 10,000 square feet of the building.

We also cherry-picked lawyers so we could work with specialists. These experts were so skilled in their target areas that our expenses were lower than if we had gone with generalist lawyers. We used one lawyer for setting up our company, one for the investigation by federal authorities, one for intellectual property assessments, and another for employee issues.

We ended up bringing on the attorney who helped us with the FBI investigation as a full-time employee, another example of our desire to build long-term, strategic partnerships.

And then there was the relationship with the jet-leasing company! One time, Mike and I had to get ourselves to Leominster, Massachusetts, in a hurry so we could meet with a customer. As we sat in our friend's Lear jet en route to Massachusetts, Mike and I fell in lust with the idea of getting around in a private jet. Within minutes, we decided that the ability to hop on a plane and quickly get anywhere was a game-changer. We giddily threw around the pros and cons of having access to our own private plane.

Not long afterward, we bought a King Air propeller plane and made nearby Burke Lakefront Airport our home airport. This whetted our appetite for quick, easy travel. We traded in the prop plane for a jet and decided to use a management company to manage it, giving us access to other planes if ours was out for maintenance. "If we're going to be heavy on relationships and provide true solutions, we need to be in front of the customer all the time," I said to Mike.

The concrete benefits were unparalleled. I once flew to South Bend, Indiana, had breakfast with a customer, flew to a remote town in Iowa, had an early lunch with another customer, then flew to McPherson, Kansas, to visit a customer in the early afternoon, and on to a fourth place for a mid-afternoon meeting and a fifth place for dinner, returning to Cleveland the next morning. I did in 24 hours with a private plane what would have taken three or four days on a commercial airliner.

We always brought along ColorMatrix employees to help develop our business and strengthen client relationships. We might have a customer who ordered our product by phone, talking to the same customer service rep day in and day out for years. Normally, our customer service rep would never meet or see the customer, but with our own jet, our clients and employees could put a face to a name. We used it as a tool to build solid relationships with our customers.

"It definitely supports our SALES FIRST! approach," Mike said, and SALES FIRST! was concrete to us, which made jet leasing and ownership a reasonable investment.

CHAPTER 24

Coca-Cola

MIKE

After his initial success, Dave McBride decided to double down on the PET industry because it was growing so quickly. Consumers wanted convenience for their on-the-go lifestyles, which included growing numbers of microwave ovens that handled PET plastic as well. The industry was a $20- to $30-billion annual market globally.

Dave visited the firm that made the packaging for Palmolive Sensitive Skin. When PET is recycled, it yellows. Colgate-Palmolive wanted to be able to use recycled PET for its Sensitive Skin bottle, but so far had been unable to do so because of the yellowing. They were working on solving this problem with their packaging supplier and a PET packaging consulting firm.

Our technical team thought they could develop a product that would do what was needed. We did trials and determined a violet toner could remove the yellowing effect in recycled PET, but to have confidence, we needed to test it specifically in the customer's machines and settings. The consultants and packaging supplier told us to give it a shot, so we customized a formula for Palmolive Sensitive Skin and experimented at its production plant near Cambridge, Ohio. The violet toner worked, which made the consultants and packaging company very happy.

Impressed with Dave's resourcefulness, the PET packaging consulting firm introduced us to a couple of their biggest clients, the bottlers for Coca-Cola. Companies, which in the industry were called "converters," made the PET bottles for two of Coca Cola's largest bottlers.

Dave said, "Western Container is located in Texas, and Southeastern Container is in North Carolina, and when these converters change from running a line producing Sprite (in a green bottle) to Coke (in a clear bottle), the line has to go through a complete color change."

This was a perfect situation for our liquid color concentrate. With their pellet-based system, machine operators had to clean out the green color from the hopper, load new resin, and wait 6-8 hours for the new resin to dry properly before they began making bottles.

John said, "Multiply this process across all the Coca-Cola products and a whole bunch of injection-molding machines and . . ." He started to do the calculations.

"You get major inefficiency," I said while he was calculating.

"Using pellets is causing this converter huge machine downtime," Dave added.

John finished his calculations and gave us the numbers. "They are throwing money out the windows!"

We installed a metering device that pumped colorant through a tube into the feed throat where the resin came into the press. Suddenly, the changeover from a Sprite line to a Coke line became this easy: the line operator or colorist turned a dial to let out color or to stop it. That's it! They could switch from green Sprite bottles to clear Coke bottles with one simple step, avoiding the machine cleaning and resin drying processes. The value proposition of reducing the number of steps in the process—and the time and labor involved—was a no-brainer.

Dave won the sale. Coca-Cola sold a lot of beverages and wanted our color system used for every Coke bottle that had color—thousands of pounds of color annually.

At work, we had to organize ourselves for growth. With the new PET business taking off, we divided our company into three markets:

- Injection-molded consumer products like flowerpots and trash cans,
- Construction and building products like PVC pipe and vinyl siding, and
- PET packaging products like juice, tea, beer, water, and ketchup bottles.

This new organization structured us for the growth that was coming at us constantly. Luckily, Dave was on a roll and continued to help us take advantage of the growing plastic packaging market.

CHAPTER 25

Glossy Flyers

JOHN

I nitially, ColorMatrix sold customers on the notion of our features and benefits. One of our first glossy flyers highlighted the accomplishments of liquid colorant, basically shouting (because we couldn't afford to be subtle), "DISPENSES COLORANT CONSISTENTLY AND INEXPENSIVELY!" Another brochure showed off our dispensing system: "PROVIDED AS A SIMPLE SYSTEM!"

In meetings with customers, I pulled out the flyers and did the back-of-the-envelope calculations I loved.

"Say you're paying $250,000 for solid color concentrate. Our liquid system will cost you $175,000 or less. That's 30 percent savings or more."

Liquid concentrate had a higher per unit price, but companies would use less liquid than dry concentrate. I showed them the *entire value proposition* of liquid colorant.

Eager to gain market share, I initially focused on cost and entered us into too many bidding wars. The few liquid colorant companies that existed—Ferro, Bee Chemical, and Riverdale—sold mainly on price alone and accepted low margins. They responded to requests for quotations (RFQs) from prospects that only wanted lower prices. Typically, a handful of competitors vied for these bids through a series of phone calls, back and forth—a pure price war. This was a commodity situation, with our competitors' chosen business model being to focus on price.

Soon enough, we figured out we wanted relationships, not price wars.

"We've gotta move away from talking about features, benefits, and cost savings," Mike said in one of our meetings after a bidding war. "We need to avoid these competitive bid situations like the plague."

We decided to make sure our SALES FIRST! approach was about not commodity selling but, instead, solutions selling. We changed our target customer to those companies that would gain eminently clear value from converting to liquid colorants. This conversion process took six to twelve months, which was eons, but the relationships we built with these customers were deep, meaningful, and enduring. For instance, one of our customers made garden supplies and had a plant in a Cleveland suburb. We converted them to liquid color in 1984, and they remained a customer for decades.

"We will never let anyone else become our liquid color supplier," an employee of the company told me several times over the years.

We figured out we didn't need glossy flyers showing off our products to make our case with the types of customers we wanted. We needed to be in front of them so we could build relationships with them. This made us completely different from our competitors. When we were in front of prospects, we could show that we knew the plastics industry incredibly well. We understood PET (food packaging), PVC (vinyl siding and pipes), and traditional injection-molded plastic products. We had our own in-house machines, and we tested products constantly so our salespeople could sell in a consultative, technical way.

CHAPTER 26

Solutions Selling

JOHN

Another example of our solutions selling method is that of a Texas company that manufactured PVC pipe and conduit. We desperately wanted to secure them as a customer, but as we were courting them, they told us they dual-sourced their materials and supplies. This means they bought materials from two suppliers instead of one so that they could establish relationships and transaction histories with both suppliers. Dual sourcing reduces a company's supply-chain risk.

"The problem with dual sourcing for liquid color is that there are no other suppliers anywhere close to us in technical sophistication," Mike said to them. "We have our own dispensing system, and we customize your formulations in customized resins, which other companies don't do, so it's going to be impossible for you to dual source this product."

"We can waive our dual-source requirement," their purchasing person told us, "but we cannot depend on your single plant location." They were concerned that if our facility experienced a disaster, then they wouldn't have any colorant supply.

"How about if we add a facility?" I asked him. "That way, if our Ohio facility becomes incapacitated due to unforeseen disaster, we can supply you from our other facility. Plus, you can always purchase a year's supply of liquid colorant from us. That's enough to last through any potential business disruption scenario I can think of."

They agreed this made sense. For us, adding a new facility for one customer was a big concession, but we were already considering doing this anyway before the customer required it.

"A second location would give most of our customers greater peace of mind," Mike had said to me a couple times, asking me to consider the possibility.

We had basically been waiting for a customer to ask for another facility so we could justify this strategy, since our SALES FIRST! mentality dictated that we couldn't add a facility until a customer asked us to do so.

This particular company wanted our second facility to be located near its operation, so we negotiated a long-term lease of a 48,000-square-foot facility that included manufacturing and lab space in Fort Worth, Texas. A few of our people transferred to Texas, but we hired mostly new people for the facility.

"This is great because it brings us closer to Mexico and the Southwest," Mike said. Both regions were high-growth plastics regions, and we were branching out beyond the Ohio Valley.

Still, the location had issues: a tornado hit Fort Worth and blew the roof off our facility shortly after we opened it, resulting in severe damage. Water destroyed many pallets of pigments. We salvaged enough pigment and equipment to resume operations within a few days.

"It's sort of funny that the plant we opened specifically to reduce risk for our customers was hit by a tornado," I offered up.

Mike wasn't amused. But the crisis did show a commitment to solving customers' problems that went far beyond a glossy brochure or responding to an RFQ. That's how we wanted to do business. We focused on the value proposition of how our entire colorant solution increased performance and quality for customers while decreasing their cost.

(John) I grew up in in Kinbrae, Minnesota, population, 29. I lived in a modest house without plumbing and used this outhouse until I was 16 years old.

(Mike) I studied hard and worked as a grocery clerk to help pay for my education at St. Louis University. My mother's unwavering belief in me contributed to my work ethic, success, and a life-long desire to help others who are less fortunate.

(Mike) The sales team at Cincinnati Milacron Chemical ~1975, where I (front row, second from right) hired John (second row, second from left). We covered sales territories together and became good friends.

Cincinnati Milacron was one of the most dynamic companies in the specialty chemicals industry. Many people there ended up as mentors, customers, and supporters of ours later. Top left: Mike; top right: John; Bottom: Mike and John in center.

Memo

To	From
G. Oleinik	M. R. Shaughnessy ✔
	Location
	Cleveland
	Date
	April 21, 1978
	Subject
	Resignation

This confirms our telephone conversation of April 18 and subsequent meeting of April 20 at which time I tendered my resignation from CINCINNATI MILACRON CHEMICALS, INC. By mutual agreement, the effective date of my resignation will be Sunday, April 23, 1978.

This will also serve to inform you that all company properties, including files, are located at 22035 Chagrin Blvd., Cleveland, Ohio. Only material of personal belonging was removed on my departure.

Please convey my best wishes for success to all of my associates at CINCINNATI MILACRON CHEMICALS. It is with high regard for their association that I will remember the company.

Respectfully,

M. R. Shaughnessy

lal

(Mike) By resigning from Cincy Milacron, I took a step toward becoming my own man, professionally. John joined me a year later, and our partnership was rock-solid, unbroken, and incredible for over 25 years.

ROSEMAR INDUSTRIES OF OHIO, INC.

Liquid Color For The Plastics Industry
45 OAKSHORE DRIVE • CLEVELAND, OHIO 44108
(216) 229-3872

October 6, 1980

FINANCIAL STATEMENT FISCAL YEAR Oct. 1,1979-Sept. 30,1980

GROSS SALES & COMMISSIONS including Accounts Receivable		$69,303.37
EXPENSES:		
Raw Materials, (including Accounts Payable)	$50,830.68	
Pumps	742.50	
Freight	1,784.49	
Travel & Entertainment	7,838.64	
Bad Debt, Returned Goods	2,576.17	
Services (Legal, Financial)	1,450.00	
Telephone & Secretarial	2,503.13	
Office Supplies	572.25	
Gifts & Donations	137.50	
Insurance	372.30	
Prepaid 1980 Income Taxes	300.00	
Salary	-0-	
	$69,107.66	
NET PROFIT		$195.71

We were realistic and specific about cash inflows and timing. We couldn't take out salaries for ourselves early on, so it was a good thing we had our sales rep business—it paid our bills and allowed us to avoid taking on outside equity.

ROSEMAR INDUSTRIES OF OHIO, INC.

Liquid Color For The Plastics Industry
45 OAKSHORE DRIVE • CLEVELAND, OHIO 44108
(216) 229-3872

Sales Forecast - Profit   Sales price minus Raw material + Container cost.

Customer	Products	Forecast lbs	Sale $	Gross margin
Carlon	75-080-1	35,000	2.70	49,350
''	45-002-5	20,000	5.91	64,600
''	77-076-1	20,000	1.32	7,400
Davies CAN	41-007-1	35,000	1.19	6650
	73-085-2			2500
	72-072-1	2,000		
	75-086-1			
	42-002-1			
Frankel	72-057-1	7500	2.26	9675
Arrow	41-005-1	24,000	2.00	27,120
	41-002-1	10,000	1.25	5,000
	72-035-1	4,000	2.42	6280
	76-071-1	1500	3.00	2775
	42-002-1	2000	1.60	1800
Freedom Plast...	74-122-3	30,000	3.45	57,000
Royal	71-069-1	4500	1.85	4230
Satar	42-006-1	18,000	1.87	10,440
Dover	81-008-1	15,000	2.55	26,250
Polycraft	72-172-1	2,000	1.80	2,000
	85-001-1	3,000	2.10	3750
	81-002-2	1000	2.22	1470
Quikut	77-073-3	5000	3.25	11,000

~ 240,000 #'s $ 299,290

From day one, our sales forecasts were bare-bones but specific, reflecting tangible customer commitments.

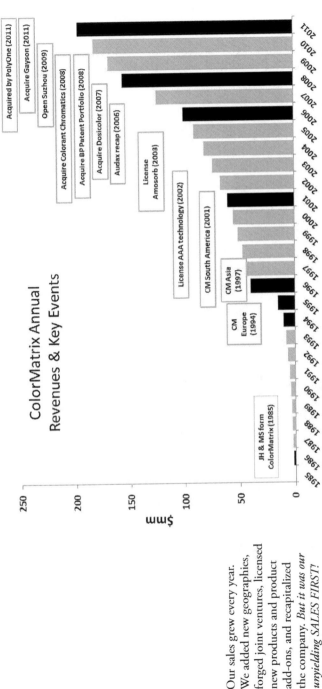

ColorMatrix Annual Revenues & Key Events

\$mm (250, 200, 150, 100, 50, 0)

Years: 1985, 1986, 1987, 1988, 1989, 1990, 1991, 1992, 1993, 1994, 1995, 1996, 1997, 1998, 1999, 2000, 2001, 2002, 2003, 2004, 2005, 2006, 2007, 2008, 2009, 2010, 2011

Key Events:
- JH & MS form ColorMatrix (1985)
- CM Europe (1994)
- CM Asia (1997)
- License AAA technology (2002)
- CM South America (2001)
- License Amosorb (2003)
- Audax recap (2006)
- Acquire Dosicolor (2007)
- Acquire BP Patent Portfolio (2008)
- Acquire Colorant Chromatics (2008)
- Open Suzhou (2009)
- Acquire Gayson (2011)
- Acquired by PolyOne (2011)

Note: To create this chart, we provided black columns for the years where ColorMatrix sales were available in public documents such as news articles, etc. The remaining columns are based on trend lines and are illustrative only.

Our sales grew every year. We added new geographies, forged joint ventures, licensed new products and product add-ons, and recapitalized the company. *But it was our unyielding SALES FIRST! approach that was the heart and soul of our growth for many years.*

JULY 25, 1997

I DID CHECK ON THOSE TWO MONTH'S
AND

BUT IT
CAR
WH

I K
MIKE
I'V
THIN

TO   MIKE :   CK 6109
                                        2/18/86
FROM   ████████████   MM
                                        WSU~

MIKE I HOPE THAT YOU HAD
    A NICE WEEKEND

JULY 25, 1997

HELLO   MIKE · SHAUGHNESSY
████████████████████████

I HAVE A BIG   PROBLEM WITH MY CAR
ON JULY 19, 1997 HUNINGTON BANK TOWED MY
CAR AWAY BECAUSE THEY THOUGHT THAT I
HAD NO INSURANCE ON THE VEHICLE, I
HAVE PROVIDED PROOF OF INSURANCE WITH
ALL STATE. THEIR SAYING THAT THERE
WAS TWO ▓▓▓ MONTH'S IN WHICH I DID
NOT HAVE INSURANCE ON THE VEHICLE.
THOSE MONTH'S WERE APRIL AND MAY.
AND THE BANK FORCED SOME OF THEIR
OWN CAR INSURANCE ON MY CAR.
IN ORDER FOR ME TO GET MY CAR OUT
OF STORAGE I'LL HAVE TO PAY FOR
THE MONTH'S THAT I DID NOT HAVE
INSURANCE. ▓▓▓▓▓▓▓ NOW BECAUSE
I'LL GET ▓▓▓ PAID TODAY I WILL
HAVE SOME OF THE MONEY THAT'S
▓▓▓▓▓▓▓ NEEDED TODAY. I HAVE
$320.00 I'▓ WILL NEED $450.00
FROM YOU, IF YOU CAN HELP ME OUT
THIS IS THE ONLY WAY I CAN GET MY
CAR BACK.

THANKS FOR EVERY THING MIKE IT REALLY
MEANS A LOT.

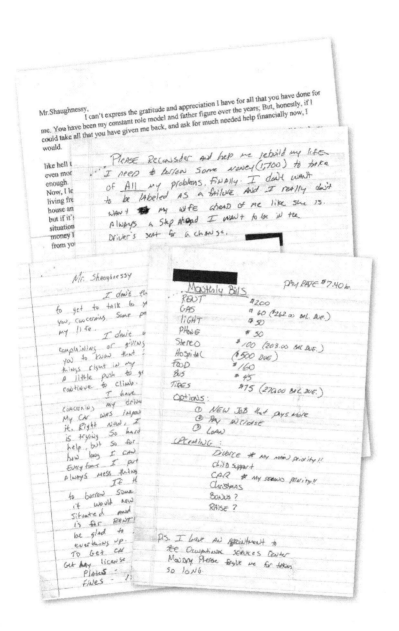

Mr. Shaughnessy,

I can't express the gratitude and appreciation I have for all that you have done for me. You have been my constant role model and father figure over the years; But, honestly, if I could take all that you have given me back, and ask for much needed help financially now, I would.

like hell t...
even mor...
enough.
Now, I le...
living fr...
house an...
but if it'...
situation...
money I...
from yo...

PLEASE Reconsider and help me rebuild my life. I need to borrow some money (1,700) to take care of ALL my problems. FINALLY. I don't want to be labeled as a failure. And I really don't want ▮ my wife ahead of me like she is. ALWAYS A step ahead. I want to be in the Driver's seat for a change.

Mr. Shaughnessy

I don't th...
to get to talk to y...
you, concerning some p...
my life.
I don't w...
complaining or giving...
you to know that...
things right in my...
a little push to g...
continue to climb.
I have...
concerning my driv...
My car was impor...
it. Right now, I...
is trying so hard...
help, but so far...
how long I can...
Every time I put...
always mess thing...
If h...
to borrow some...
it would now...
situated and...
is for RENT!...
be glad to...
everthing up...
To get car...
Get my license...
Plates -...
Fines - 1...

▮   PAY RATE $7.40 hr

.Monthly Bills
RENT $200
GAS $60 ($262.00 bal. due)
LIGHT $50
PHONE $50
Stereo $100 ($303.00 bal. due)
Hospital   ($500 due)
FOOD $160
Bus $45
TIRES $75 ($270.00 bal. due)

OPTIONS:
① NEW JOB that pays more
② PAY increase
③ LOAN

UPCOMING:
   DIVORCE # my main priority!!
   Child support
   CAR # my second priority!!
   Christmas
   Bonus?
   Raise?

P.S. I have an appointment to see Occupational Services Center Monday Please forgive me for taken so long.

Employees often came to us with needs in their personal lives, and we usually responded. We tried to help them break lifelong, poor financial habits—sometimes successfully and sometimes not.

The lobby of Colormatrix Corp.'s new headquarters displays a variety of products in which the company's liquid colors are used. Chief Executive Officer John Haugh, right, and President Michael Shaughnessy, left, own the Cleveland company.

Giving the world a brighter hue

Colormatrix decides to stay in Cleveland

By BECKY YERAK
PLAIN DEALER REPORTER

Colormatrix Corp., a mainstay in the city of Cleveland since it was founded 12 years ago, was courted by suburbs as well as Tennessee, Missouri and Wisconsin when word got out that it sorely needed more space.

But the rapidly growing supplier of liquids used to color a wide range of plastics chose to stay in the Midtown Corridor, the economically struggling area stretching from E. 22nd St. to the Cleveland Clinic.

Partly lured by the carrot of tax breaks, it has leased 70,000 square feet in the old Wirtshafter's Building at 3005 Chester Ave., nearly five times more space than it had at its former facility at 4133 Payne Ave.

"Our work pool is predominantly people who live in the inner city," said Michael Shaughnessy, who, with John Haugh, owns Colormatrix.

Nearly a third of its workers rely on public transportation to get to work. In just the past seven months, Colormatrix

has grown from 36 to 56 workers, most of them in Cleveland.

In recent years, the company has relied on Cleveland Works Inc. — which turns welfare recipients into taxpayers — to help fill its growing ranks. A few workers who started with GEDs now have college degrees, made possible through Colormatrix's educational assistance program. It also lets workers have a piece of the action through a profit-sharing plan.

"Cleveland has been good to us," Shaughnessy said. "We wanted to stay in the city. We see a lot of exciting things happening downtown."

The new space should accommodate Colormatrix's growth for the next five years, Haugh said. Sales will exceed $15 million this year, up 50% from a year ago.

The company recently added a shift and is running 24 hours a day, five days a week. "In the last five years, we've not seen a year with less than 25% growth," he added.

Colormatrix supplies liquid colorants

to businesses that make the plastic bottles for such products as Coke, Pepsi and 7 Up. Although it has been slashing its number of suppliers, Rubbermaid Inc. recently asked Colormatrix to supply colors for a line of storage containers.

Lamson & Sessions Co., which makes pipes for construction and electrical industries, is one of its oldest and best customers. And Royal Appliance Manufacturing Co. and J.M. Smucker Co. also use its products.

In the plastics colorant industry, liquid colors now account for 15% to 20% of the market, with the rest from, say, powders or pellets, Shaughnessy said. The three leading U.S. liquid color companies are Colormatrix, Cleveland's Ferro Corp. and Morton International, he added.

Colormatrix also is seeing some long-term work come to fruition.

For example, vinyl siding colored with its products had to undergo years of weatherability testing. Colormatrix's relatively small and nimbler size, and growing foreign markets, also are behind the boost in business.

Cleveland had inexpensive manufacturing space, strong public transport, and (once we figured out how to harness it) a dedicated workforce. We loved this combination and believe the city of Cleveland helped us vitally with much of our successful growth.

In addition to SALES FIRST!, we loved polymer science and color chemistry. Fortunately, they were part of a $6 billion plastic additives market, which meant we could turn our skills and our fields of interest into a thriving business.

CRAIN'S
CLEVELAND BUSINESS

CRAINSCLEVELAND.COM | OCTOBER 3, 2011 |

MANUFACTURING

PolyOne Corp. agrees to acquire ColorMatrix Group Inc. for $486 million

One Cleveland-area company has agreed to buy another in a $486 million deal. Polymer producer PolyOne Corp. (NYSE: POL) in Avon Lake plans to acquire ColorMatrix Group Inc., a supplier of liquid colorants, additives and fluoropolymers that is based in Berea. According to PolyOne, ColorMatrix had sales of nearly $197 million and earnings before interest, taxes, depreciation and amortization (EBITDA) of $43.6 million in the 12 months that ended last June 30. "Since 2002, ColorMatrix has organically increased EBITDA at an annualized growth rate of 16%, and our purchase price of $486 million recognizes the earnings and growth potential of this specialty business," Stephen Newlin, PolyOne chairman, president and CEO, said in a statement. Mr. Newlin said PolyOne officials "believe we can accelerate this growth by leveraging our global scale and through additional investment in commercial resources" at ColorMatrix. Mr. Newlin said the addition of ColorMatrix means more than 50% of PolyOne's operating income now will be derived from its specialty businesses, "compared to only 2% in 2005." Robert M. Patterson,

PolyOne executive vice president and chief financial officer, said the acquisition of ColorMatrix not only will accelerate its specialization strategy, "it also expands our geographic presence in Asia and Brazil and creates an entry point into Russia." About 70% of ColorMatrix's revenues are outside North America, according to PolyOne. PolyOne said it intends to finance the purchase price of $486 million, which includes transaction tax benefits of $10 million, with a combination of cash on hand and the addition of approximately $300 million of long-term debt. "Net of interest expense on the long-term debt, and the incremental investments in commercial resources, we expect ColorMatrix to be modestly accretive to earnings in 2012 (by two cents to three cents a share) and to add approximately 10 cents to 12 cents per share in 2013," Mr. Patterson said. PolyOne said the acquisition is subject to regulatory approvals and is expected to close late this year. PolyOne said its management will discuss the acquisition in more detail during its regularly scheduled third-quarter earnings conference call set for Oct. 26.

When PolyOne acquired ColorMatrix, our journey in liquid colorants ended. We felt proud and humbled that over 25 years, we had somehow strung together successes, created jobs, and changed an industry.

CHAPTER 27

Goal: $100 Million

JOHN

$$\left[\begin{array}{c} CH_3 \\ | \\ O-C-O \\ | \\ H \end{array} \begin{array}{c} O \\ \| \\ \\ \end{array} \right]_n$$

Eventually, our primary strategy crystallized:
- Use the SALES FIRST! approach.
- Build enduring relationships, which add to our values and became our culture.
- Sell complete solutions—don't commoditize.

This worked well for us. The hardest part of our growth curve was reaching $1 million because we had to build credibility to get early sales. Then we grew from $1 million in annual revenue in the early 1980s to about $10 million by 1993. We brought on a couple dozen new customers per year and continually pried open the market for liquid colorants. From 1991-2000, we made the Weatherhead 100 list of fastest-growing businesses in Northeast Ohio every year. In 1995, we also won the Ernst & Young Entrepreneur of the Year Award. These honors made us proud.

Yet we wanted more.

"I think in this market, we can grow to $100 million," Mike said.

"You think so?"

"I know we can. I think we've got to go after that goal."

India and China were becoming major forces in the plastics industry. Global companies with professional purchasing managers were replacing the dying breed of small plastics processors. And we were selling into the leading edge of that change.

"Not taking on outside investors is going to put a damper on our growth," Mike said, "but I think we can grow quickly without investors."

We continued to toe the line of being high-growth entrepreneurs and yet bootstrappers too. We were adamant about being self-financed and independent. Fortunately, timing was on our side. In the early 1980s when we started out, the plastics colorant market was worth hundreds of millions of dollars annually and almost entirely made up of solid-color concentrate. By 2004, the global plastics colorant market reached $5.7 billion with liquid colorant's growth rate at twice that of dry colorants.

With that kind of market growth, we went from living paycheck-to-paycheck to running a successful, rapidly growing business.

CHAPTER 28

European Partners

MIKE

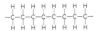

I met Bill Ravenna in the early 1990s when he was a sales-person for American Cyanamid, a diversified company that made pharmaceuticals, building products, and specialty chemicals. He called me to sell us ultraviolet (UV) absorber. As we talked, he revealed that he wanted to leave his current employer and start a business in England with two other guys.

Mark Frost and Dave Nuttall were the "other guys." All three had majored in chemical engineering at various universities and had met as MBA students at the University of Manchester. In a damp corner in upper western England, they had developed a pact that someday they'd start a business.

"Bill seems really capable. I'd love to support him in his dreams," I told John. We were thinking about getting into the European market, and I thought Bill might represent the opportunity for us to do that.

John, Dave McBride, and I had heard European PET processors were moving to on-site coloring systems.

"Why doesn't Bill Ravenna go over to England and look into that for us?" John suggested.

I threw out this idea to Bill, who was living in the US, and he liked it. He commissioned a study from some students at University of Manchester and ultimately secured a company called Constar as a first customer. With that, Bill moved to the UK, and we inked a ten-year agreement with him, Dave, and Mark for the formation of ColorMatrix Europe. This company licensed know-how and purchased materials from us on favorable payment terms. In exchange, we received royalties on sales of liquid colorant.

In our partnerships, we stressed the importance of a structure and culture of equality, as well as having backstops in case of failure of the partnership. We set up the partnership as an export arrangement under which we exported the licensed product to ColorMatrix Europe, and they distributed it. We didn't invest big money in building new manufacturing facilities or making acquisitions. Our manufacturing remained in the US. A second step, if all went well, would be to set up manufacturing in Europe.

We wanted to be for our European partners what Gary Curtiss had been for us—guys who removed barriers for others—and I think we succeeded. Bill, Mark, and Dave started tinkering in a headquarters location (i.e., the apartment building where Bill lived) in a village near Manchester. We sent them materials in five-gallon quantities, and they sampled, tested, and repackaged them to test with customers. They found the opportunities, we provided technical support and produced colorants and additives, and they priced and resold them under the ColorMatrix Europe brand.

CHAPTER 29

Opportunists

MIKE

Eventually, Bill, Mark, and Dave set up office space in Knowsley, England, which had created an economic development zone to combat the employment devastation of coal mines that had closed across northern England. Bill, the American, was a bit of a cowboy and had a commercial orientation. He became our European sales leader. David was operational and administrative, running the company's day-to-day business. And Mark was a strong technologist, technically sound and creative. Dave's and Mark's detail orientation nicely complemented Bill's big-picture salesmanship.

It wasn't always sunshine and roses among us all. Early on, Bill, Dave, and Mark wanted to sell as "ColourMatrix" because that spelling of "color" was more familiar to Europeans.

We understood their desire to "do as the Romans do," but for branding purposes, we wanted them to sell as "ColorMatrix." They weren't happy. (Plus, they had already ordered ColourMatrix signage and stationery.) Another time, Bill, Dave, and Mark concluded that they wanted to enter the PVC extrusion (pipe and vinyl siding) and injection molding markets. We sold into these markets in the US and knew they were commodity businesses with deteriorating profit margins.

"The packaging market is much higher margin," I said.

"Why do you want to sell into low-margin markets when we haven't exploited even a small part of the packaging market?" John asked.

They did not agree with our request to avoid the PVC market, but over the ensuing years, they at least respected and heeded it. We all agreed that we wanted to compete with great relationships and systemic solutions to customer problems, not with low prices. For years, John and I had lived the reality that our market-focused, non-commodity strategy required discipline—most of all when it meant passing up big-revenue opportunities.

One time, a South African company wanted them to provide liquid color concentrate for the fiber used in fabrics. For technical reasons, we could only consistently predict the final color of a fiber by investing in expensive machinery, which we didn't want to do, especially without a large commitment from a customer. However, ColorMatrix Europe spent about $200,000 on a fiber spinning machine and lab equipment to do development work without getting a purchase order first.

When we heard about it, John and I were taken aback. This wasn't our SALES FIRST! approach.

"We don't sell into that industry. Why are you spending money there?" I nearly yelled into the phone.

"It's a big market and uses the same polymer," Bill said.

He couldn't believe we were going to ignore an opportunity to develop a huge market that he had long been cultivating. ColorMatrix Europe was growing at about $1.5 million per year—a meaningful addition to our US revenue—and Bill and his partners were confident operators.

"But we're supposed to be focusing on the packaging industry," John said. "And we don't have enough experience in fiber."

The Europeans, on the other hand, loved the technical challenge.

The episode spoke to the largest area of friction between us and ColorMatrix Europe. Bill, David, and Mark were contemporary extensions of the UK's pioneering of color chemistry. As idea guys and innovators, they wanted to invest up-front to develop products that had a need down the road, and sometimes wanted to move into markets ahead of sales and revenue.

Meanwhile, as sales guys and opportunists, Mike and I obsessed about running the business using a SALES FIRST! mentality. We compulsively avoided the "if we build it, they will come" approach, and we saw any movement toward needing investor capital as a step away from the financial independence that we had always considered sacrosanct. We absolutely had to control our own destiny.

CHAPTER 30

Great Partners

JOHN

$$\left[O-\underset{\underset{H}{|}}{\overset{\overset{CH_3}{|}}{C}}-\overset{O}{\overset{\|}{C}}-O \right]_n$$

Despite occasional disagreements with our European partners, we maintained a strong partnership because one thing above all others makes a joint venture a success: performance. These guys performed every step of the way! They surpassed $500,000 in revenue in their first year and reached about $2 million in their second year—a growth rate that helped smooth out our differing entrepreneurship philosophies.

Another time, Eastman Chemical in Europe offered a great opportunity. The company wanted to shed its resin service center equipment and employees. Bill Ravenna had an idea.

"I think we should acquire the equipment," he said.

The equipment included machines for running color matches and production-scale, multiple-cavity molds that could get us into extruding and molding finished products for our customers in Europe. These capabilities could distance us from our commodity-based competitors and aligned well with our commitment to solution selling.

"I think this is a great decision. Let's do it," I said.

Bill, Mark, and Dave bought the equipment, which was not inexpensive, set it up as a service center in Eindhoven, Netherlands, and began providing services. When Coca-Cola wanted to sponsor the World Cup soccer competition and run hundreds of thousands of bottles with promotional colors, we did this for them. That made Coke happy because it didn't want to interrupt its high-volume manufacturing lines for a short run. The Coke team came to our facility and spent a day completing the run, which saved them money and built our relationship. Other times, our Netherlands service center remixed colorant for customers. Remix is required after liquid colorants settle from sitting on a shelf too long. Our customer could ship the settled colorant to our newly acquired Netherlands facility, where our lab technicians remixed it and sent it back to the customer.

Our European team's instincts on taking advantage of the opportunity to acquire that facility had been right on. It helped us forge even stronger relationships with our customers in Europe.

"They are great partners for us," John said. "You know, they probably structure their operations and manage people better than we do."

CHAPTER 31

Entering Asia

MIKE

We wanted to copy and paste our ColorMatrix Europe experience in other geographies, namely Asia. The Asian tiger was fully upon the plastics industry, with Asia taking enormous market share from US companies. Further, its consumer class was growing so that it also had domestic demand.

On one trip to the UK, Dave McBride met someone who could help us in Asia: Ben Chan, a Canadian of Chinese descent. As he and Dave talked, Ben disclosed that he had a close relationship with the head of a large company that made preforms and bottles for Coca-Cola bottlers in China.

"Wow, that's great, because we're already an approved supplier within the Coca-Cola system," Dave said.

The combination of Ben's connection plus our approved-supplier status plus China's massive growth led them to one conclusion: ColorMatrix should pursue the Chinese market as soon as possible.

"Ben, do you think you can help us land this converter as a customer?" I asked him.

"I think so," he replied.

He developed an opportunity large enough that it prompted us to set up a new joint venture, ColorMatrix Asia. As 25-percent owner of the venture, Ben moved to Hong Kong to run it. Great Britain still governed Hong Kong, so our Hong Kong company could legally be set up like a British company.

I always wanted us to make exporting from the US our first step to each new market entry and then make the second step, if successful, the notion of setting up manufacturing.

"We're on step one of our two-step process," I reminded our team, so they knew we could take this further if we wanted.

We mixed the liquid colorant and produced the dispensing system in Cleveland and shipped the products to our ColorMatrix Hong Kong warehouse, receiving payment in US dollars. ColorMatrix Asia used a customs broker to ship the colorant products to the converter, which was based in Wan Chai, an impressive industrial complex on the border of Hong Kong.

The PET market in China interested us because, compared to other types of plastics (e.g., polypropylene, polyethylene, etc.), PET had more proprietary formulas, greater innovation, and higher margins. Ben relied on his far-reaching personal network and ability to speak Mandarin to secure new PET packaging business for us. He had spent a good part of his twenty-or-so-year career selling for a huge company in the injection molding machine industry, so he was used to being at a company that was the 800-pound gorilla in its industry.

Things changed for him when he began working with

us in China and couldn't rely on the status of working with a large, known, brand-name company. At the same time, South Korean commodities companies started flooding Hong Kong and China. They successfully replaced Color-Matrix Asia's customers at low prices. As a successful, disciplined commercial salesman, Ben resented this Korean influx. He desperately wanted to avoid commoditizing ColorMatrix Asia, so he found great ways to hit back hard at the South Korean commodities companies by partnering us with a Korean businessman who knew the South Korean colorant market.

This excited John, who predicted, "With these guys, we're going to beat the South Koreans at their own game. This is great!"

Indeed, Ben and the colorants expert were able to sell our liquid colorant systems into South Korea with surprising success, landing customer after customer. They showed the South Koreans that ColorMatrix could one-up them. Meanwhile, Ben taught us an important lesson on how to compete in Asian markets.

CHAPTER 32

South America

MIKE

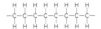

We wanted more joint ventures, and next up was South America. We wanted to start in Brazil, the most populous country in South America. Canadian Dean Miller served as our conduit. He had a real gift for languages; using no guides or teachers, he had taught himself Portuguese so well that within six months, he could fully converse with Brazilians.

On our behalf, Dean gained familiarity with the Brazilian market for liquid colorants. He then found converter customers and devised a plan for us to generate revenue from each one. We thought his analysis was great, and with him and a husband-wife couple who became our equity partners in Brazil, we created a new joint venture. ColorMatrix-Brazil would sell liquid colorants to companies, primarily converters, located in Brazil. We had the two equity partners, but Dean, who lived near São Paulo, became our "feet on the street."

We modeled our Brazilian outpost after our Color-Matrix Asia and ColorMatrix Europe joint ventures. We did up-front technical work running trials and produced colorant systems in Cleveland and then sent them to Brazil. Our partners warehoused the systems, marked up their prices, and sold them to customers. We also formed a second South American joint venture, ColorMatrix South America, which was a British Virgin Islands company that allowed us to export legally from Brazil to the rest of South America.

As we gained confidence in Europe and Brazil, we moved to step two. We licensed the manufacturing process to our partners there, and they produced colorant systems and provided technical support for customers. In Brazil, we set up our plant in Itupeva, which is called "PET Valley" because many resin producers and processors call it home.

We gained a surprising amount of satisfaction from removing hurdles for our three joint venture partnerships, de-risking our partners' early days, and helping them become experts.

"Go sell the product, and if it's not doing what you need it to do, tell us," we said to them. "We'll find a way to get it to do what you need it to."

We wanted our partners to focus on selling into the geographies they knew, and we could support everything else. In Europe, Asia, and Brazil, ColorMatrix trailblazed the liquid colorant market. Each of our partners worked closely with us to research the market and find real opportunities, so we had high confidence that brought a valued solution into the market. This fact-gathering process gave us the confidence we needed to enter new global geographies.

CHAPTER 33

TripleA Scavenger

MIKE

After Dave McBride took responsibility for our PET packaging business, he found a major bottled-water opportunity for us. When processed, PET plastic sometimes releases a harmless chemical (acetaldehyde) that can seep into food or drink and slightly affect its flavor. Food companies reduced the effects this acetaldehyde seepage had on flavor by adding antioxidants to their PET resin. Unfortunately, these antioxidants also changed the color of the resins, an acceptable side effect for colored plastic bottles but not for clear bottles. Who wants to drink water from a cloudy bottle?

The bottled water industry needed a solution to remove excess acetaldehyde without discoloring polyester. At the same time, Europe's beverage industry leaders wanted to figure out how to switch from glass to plastic water bottles, a multibillion-dollar opportunity but a challenge. Glass was the container of choice for Germans, and most European countries were similar: they preferred glass, which was expensive to make, use, and handle, and was less recyclable.

If we solved these problems, we'd make a lot of money.

Constar, one of our first European customers was racing to make clear plastic water bottles. Our ColorMatrix Europe team had forged a partnership with a few university researchers, and together with Constar, they were experimenting with ways to decrease acetaldehyde levels. They talked regularly with bottled water companies to come up with a solution.

Back in the US, we also were investigating the water bottle issue. Dave was calling on Coca-Cola, whose bottlers were some of our largest customers. Coca-Cola was developing its Dasani line of bottled water, and its research team was trying to control acetaldehyde in a project at its Atlanta corporate offices.

"Why don't I bring our head of R&D, John Standish, to meet with you, and we can talk this through together?" I asked a Coca-Cola researcher. I thought John could learn from the Dasani research team and, conversely, add his own knowledge to their project.

"What are you guys doing on acetaldehyde scavengers?" the Coca-Cola project manager asked at the meeting in Atlanta.

John told him about potential solutions being developed in the ColorMatrix Europe research project.

Dave's and John's knowledge so impressed Mark Rule, a Coca-Cola scientist, that he started to open up at the meeting about what Coca-Cola was doing.

"I've developed a decent technology," Mark said, describing how he had developed an acetaldehyde "scavenger," which was an exciting breakthrough. The men talked chemistry for a while, and Mark ended by asking John, "Would you be willing to submit your research samples to us? We can compare them to ours and see what works and what doesn't? Maybe we'll all learn something."

This was just what Dave wanted from the meeting. He called the Europeans to give them the news, and with that, ColorMatrix in Europe and the US formed an experimentation team with Coca-Cola. After a while, Mark Rule came back to us with his conclusion: the ColorMatrix research was good but not as good as what Coca-Cola had developed themselves. Its TripleA scavenger eliminated acetaldehyde diffusion in PET, entirely avoiding the problem of discoloration. It was a breakthrough by Coca-Cola.

Still, we weren't upset. We had still developed a meaningful collaboration, and Coca-Cola treated us like a valued partner.

Mark subsequently contacted Dave McBride. "We're about to patent our technology, and we are looking for someone to license it," he said. He explained that once Coca-Cola received Food and Drug Administration approval, it could use the technology in its Dasani bottled water line. But Coke knew it would make more money on its TripleA scavenger technology by getting other companies to use it.

We believed this TripleA scavenger would open up the plastic water bottle market, so we worked out a global licensing deal with Coca-Cola. Once we had the license to sell TripleA, Bill, David, and Mark in the UK made quick work of converting the German bottled water market to plastic. This was a big deal. Consumers could finally drink water from plastic PET bottles that were clear and had no effect on flavor. With this success, our sales grew at a record pace, especially in Europe, which went from 20 percent of

ColorMatrix revenue in 1996 to almost 40 percent in 2004 and then to about 50 percent in 2006.

We didn't develop TripleA ourselves, yet the market was large, and our knowledge was strong, so we made a lot of money from licensing the technology. This first experience with licensing a technology showed us that licensing could be a promising route for us. At the same time, we knew "luck favors the prepared." We never would have been in a position to license the TripleA invention without the research John Standish and the Europeans had done. At the end of the day, that is what had impressed Mark Rule.

We advanced our research and kept up with the industry.

We understood the value of what Coca-Cola had.

We knew the market size and dynamics.

As long as ColorMatrix had a presence in markets and conducted its own basic level of research and development, we showed plastics-related inventors we were well positioned to license and commercialize their new technologies.

CHAPTER 34

Amosorb

MIKE

Dave led the TripleA scavenger success, and although he was young, he became the central point for information shared between our researchers and Coca-Cola. As a small business becoming a mid-sized business, we needed managers who could deal with this transition. They needed to be independent but not so independent they went off the reservation. That's difficult to find in a manager.

Dave displayed exactly this mix. He thought and acted independently yet respected our way of growing the company. In that light, he next led another technology success for us. A lot of our PET customers were trying to make juice, tea, beer, water, and ketchup last longer in PET containers. During the first steps of packaging a food or beverage, oxygen seeps in through tiny pores and causes unwanted oxidation. The result is like when you take a bite out of an apple and it turns brown a few minutes later.

The primary way producers fixed the oxidation and discoloration was by using three layers of plastic—first PET, then nylon, then PET again. The central nylon layer created an oxygen barrier, but at a cost: Three layers of plastic was wasteful, heavy, expensive, and not very recyclable. Food and beverage companies worldwide were trying to figure out how to "light weight" plastic packaging.

Being ambitious, John Standish wanted to come up with a solution. He hired Ron Valus, who had spent his career in research at British Petroleum in Cleveland and had developed expertise in polymers and gas diffusion.

"We need to completely understand oxygen barrier technologies," John Standish said, directing Ron to work on this issue in the lab.

One day, Dave McBride and John Standish were in Atlanta visiting Mark Rule at Coca-Cola when they started talking about oxygen ingress in plastic containers. Because of the TripleA scavenger success, we felt at ease sharing our research and development. We knew Coke had engaged BP to help with the oxygen ingress problem.

"I'd like you to talk with my friend Greg Schmidt who works at BP in Chicago," Mark Rule said.

As a sharp researcher with a PhD in chemistry, Greg oversaw business development and scientific projects. John and Dave got on the phone with him, and they began talking about oxygen barriers and the work ColorMatrix had done.

"You know, we've been working on that," Greg said. "Maybe we should start talking more formally."

Greg and the chemist involved in developing a BP product called "Amosorb" flew to Cleveland. Our lab guru, Ron Valus, knew exactly how to test the BP technology, so he and the BP chemist hit it off immediately.

"Wow, you guys really know this stuff!" Greg said as he watched them at work.

As with our acetaldehyde situation, the BP and Coca-Cola researchers told us we weren't as far along as they were, but our scientists' expertise and findings impressed them. It turned out that Amosorb scavenged oxygen as a food or beverage was being packaged. This "always active" capability was a breakthrough because it meant companies didn't have to use three layers of plastic to prevent air from permeating their juice, tea, beer, water, or ketchup. They could use one lightweight plastic resin mixed with Amosorb. In addition, people could recycle plastic containers made with Amosorb.

Lightweight, cost-efficient, and recyclable: Amosorb checked all the boxes for meeting the industry's needs. Greg Schmidt knew Amosorb held a lot of promise, but he and his colleagues had sold relatively little of the material over six years, which frustrated them.

Dave McBride jumped all over this. "I am certain we can sell Amosorb," he told me.

As we talked about it, we realized that if we added Amosorb to our offerings, we'd have a great product suite:

- Complete liquid colorant systems that were better than commodity pellets and powders,
- TripleA scavengers for the bottled water industry, and
- Amosorb for packaging of perishable foods and beverages.

Dave and John Standish came to us to explain that we needed to license this technology and that the negotiations wouldn't be a slam dunk. We may have been the right partner, but BP was obliged to shop around its technology and get the best deal it could. To put us as high up on the potential partner list as possible, Dave and John developed a great licensing and commercialization plan—very bullish and confident—and shared it with Greg at BP.

Greg must have determined that ColorMatrix had the right knowledge, skills, and commercialization plan, because he recommended to BP that it offer us the Amosorb licensing opportunity. In 2003, we added Amosorb to our product line.

Unfortunately, we faced a credibility problem with our sales team because as a pellet-based product, Amosorb differed from our "all-liquid-all-the-time" position in the market. Liquid had been our founding idea and our heritage. Many times over the years, our salespeople had asked us if we could add color concentrate *pellets* to our product suite so they could sell dry color to customers who wouldn't convert to liquid.

"No," we had always said to them. "Our differentiation and positioning are that we are a liquid colorant company, and we need to keep it that way."

Now, we were seemingly reversing course, asking our salespeople to sell our customers on a pellet-based product. We knew this seemed hypocritical, but the underlying value of the Amosorb technology aligned with our positioning. We produced liquid versus solid colorant not because we had an irrational love for liquid but because its technical superiority yielded better results and higher margins for customers. Our real product differentiation had nothing to do with liquid versus solid, but rather with adding value to solve customer problems and produce high margins.

Although a pellet, Amosorb accomplished those objectives.

We explained this to our salesforce, and by and large, they

accepted it. But at the same time, we developed a liquid form of Amosorb that they could sell alongside the pellet form.

As head of our PET sales and marketing efforts, Dave McBride had owned most of the commercial aspects of our technical opportunities, so he had managed the largest portion of our business for years. We promoted him to business unit manager for packaging, and he just kept going—knocking on doors, generating new sales, and growing the company.

CHAPTER 35

See You at the Top

JOHN

$$\left[-O-\overset{\overset{\displaystyle CH_3}{|}}{\underset{\underset{\displaystyle H}{|}}{C}}-\overset{\overset{\displaystyle O}{\|}}{O}-\right]_n$$

In the initial hires we made at ColorMatrix, we didn't much focus on the skill set of relationship building. With our SALES FIRST! mentality consuming us, we hired people who could support us by keeping their heads down and doing the background work to help us sell. This worked well until it didn't.

"Our entire team needs training on how to build relationships," Mike said one day. His frustration stemmed from an employee who wasn't working well with another employee. "We have got to put something in place to help them develop relationship skills," he said.

We looked at our options and decided to use a training program based on Zig Ziglar's best-selling book, *See You at the Top*. Born a dirt-poor southerner, Ziglar eventually made a great living and became wealthy. He decided to share what he had learned about character and motivation. When it came to relationships, he had one core belief: "If you set out to make a friend, you wouldn't find many. If you set out to be a friend, you'll find them everywhere."

He felt that if people consistently gave back to their world rather than expecting something from it, they'd find success in life. A person became a friend to others through the core values of honesty, loyalty, faith, integrity, and strong personal character.

Ziglar didn't think every person came into the world with these values, but he believed that no matter what walk of life a person came from, he or she could learn them.

Ziglar's ideas matched Mike's and mine, and building great relationships based on the core values of honesty, loyalty, faith, integrity, and strong personal character essentially became our culture. We went to a "train the trainer" session in Dallas so we could learn how to teach Zig Ziglar's program to our team. When we came back, we began to use a video cassette and our training and ideas to infuse the *See You at the Top* mentality into our company.

From early on, this yielded good results. One woman who worked with us had lost her husband. He was killed in the middle of an armed robbery. She subsequently developed significant health problems, and with the stresses in her life, her confidence suffered. She had kids at home to feed, and she lived in constant fear of destitution, always worried and nervous; if you looked at her cross-eyed, she'd cry. After the *See You at the Top* course, she developed a better self-image and became much more confident. She became friends with her co-workers, practiced the core values, and used those successes to start expressing her professional needs appropriately.

"I'm working with customers, taking sample requests, performing our bookkeeping, and working as a receptionist. I do a lot of things and should be compensated differently," she said to us one day.

Her sudden forthrightness took us by surprise, but we loved that she had developed a belief in the power of her own integrity, honesty, and strong personal character, and we loved that this gave her the confidence to ask for a raise.

CHAPTER 36

Working Smarter

JOHN

At some point along our path from $10 million to $100 million, Mike and I figured out we didn't know everything we needed to know about growing a company to $100 million. We started out stupid and tried to work harder to become smart, and we became disillusioned when this "work harder" strategy didn't work.

"You know what, Mike? We need to work smarter, not harder," I said one day. "We need to hire people who are smarter than us, and people who have skill sets we don't."

If we were going to hire up, we needed to improve our organization building skills. These skills had always played second fiddle to our selling and relationship skills.

Solving technical problems: check.

Selling all the time through SALES FIRST!: check.

Building customer relationships: check.

But we despised trying to solve our own organization's people problems, and we diligently avoided being a human resources department. Employees and partners, some of whom had loads of potential, became frustrated enough with us that they left. Then we scratched our heads and wondered what had gone wrong.

"Well, we really didn't invest much in developing them," Mike might say to me.

In fact, that became a common refrain.

So I said, "Look, we've gotta find a better way of developing people. It's completely stalling our growth."

We needed to build our organization, starting with a more strategic people plan. I have to say that this was pretty painful. We knew how to spend money on equipment when a customer opportunity required that we invest. Now we had to spend money on people who weren't all going to be selling our products 100 percent of the time or helping us solve customer problems but would support our infrastructure?

Well now, *that* was hard to swallow.

CHAPTER 37

Improving Quality

JOHN

We began in 1995 by bringing in John Standish to do an overhaul of our technical capabilities. He had a BS in chemistry, a master's in material science, and PhD in polymer science and engineering, a combination of credentials that put him among the best color chemists in the industry.

"We need you to help us develop expertise that matches the expertise of our largest customers," I said.

These customers had research and development budgets in the hundreds of millions of dollars, so this was a somewhat ridiculous request. But if anyone could do it, John Standish could. He knew everything about our technical process and our customers' processes, plus he understood our SALES FIRST! approach.

"I worked as a technical salesperson at my prior company," he said, "and from that role, I understand the pressure to get products out the door to customers. Manufacturing lines don't wait for things to grow in petri dishes and for scientists to stare at them."

He knew how to conduct science projects that served real customer needs.

John Standish also set up his processes using quality control systems like Deming and ISO. These systems were only beginning to take root when Mike and I had left big-company life. In his first days on the job, John had to tell us our company needed to use these processes. Mike and I didn't know Deming and ISO at all well, but we didn't let that stop us from having an opinion, namely that we didn't care much for them.

SALES FIRST! is working for us, I thought. *Why do we need to complicate it?* (We knew we needed to build out our organization and processes but changing our thought patterns was hard.)

John Standish was a plain-spoken guy, but he didn't relish delivering bad news to us, his new bosses. "Our manufacturing operating and delivery problems can be traced back to poor quality control systems," he said. "We *have* to adopt a formal quality program."

We weren't convinced. We thought our quality was great.

He begged to differ. "Most of our customer complaints can be traced back to the core problem of our having poor quality control systems." He said that while we were out selling and growing the business, employees in the office were pointing fingers at each other about whose fault customer issue were. "If we had better tracking and control, when employees played the blame game, we could track down evidence to figure out what really was going on. It would improve employee morale," John said.

I still wasn't convinced. In fact, I was annoyed that someone who didn't know what we had been through all these years, hauling our butts to sell, was criticizing our company. I heard him out, as did Mike, but I didn't allow him to do what he wanted to do. This frustrated him because he was a systems guy who wasn't being allowed to invest in systems.

Then Mark Frost, our European partner and technology expert, joined the chorus. He started telling me the same things as John—we needed quality control experts who understood our products and our customers' equipment at a deeper level. Mark said, "We need people who know the idiosyncrasies of our products and who can help us more systematically deliver products to our customers."

So here I was in the mid-1990s, with over a decade of experience running a business that was winning awards and growing like gangbusters, hearing a steady drumbeat of how bad we were. That's how I took it, anyhow.

CHAPTER 38

Adding Depth

JOHN

I was frustrated, but they were adamant, so Mike and I acquiesced and allowed our team to invest in quality-control procedures. We also added depth to our technical capabilities in our fastest-growing market, PET food and beverage packaging. We hired Bob Prewitt, whom people revered for his skill in conducting technical audits on resin dryers. Resin that doesn't dry properly is an urgent technical problem because it shuts down a processor's line. And we hired John Bombace, who had been manager of operations for Southeastern Container, owned by Coca-Cola Bottling Company. He would lead our PET technical service group. We also added Kyle Clark, who had tremendous background in PET processing.

We also added organizational depth in other areas. To cut costs, plastics processors had shed many of their technical people, and we picked them up so we could become a centralized source of plastics industry technical skills. For instance, we hired Jim Renfro, who had been a manager at a PVC extrusion plant and knew extrusion inside and out. From then on, when we visited our extrusion customers, such as the CEO at Carlon, one of our biggest customers, Jim went along and showed them ways to improve their operations.

Beyond quality and technical specialists, we added people with operations skill sets who could help us run our business more efficiently and increase our profit margins. We promoted a color chemist, John Lesho, to run our plant and make sure we produced and delivered our colorant systems on schedule and on budget. We recruited coatings industry veteran Gerry Corrigan and asked him to figure out how we could convert scrap into saleable product. He did this and delivered bottom-line impact quickly. After he oversaw manufacturing operations for a bit, we promoted him to chief operating officer.

These hires in quality engineering, science, and operations represented major investments put distance between us and our competition. Because we had a variety of new processes, John Standish and Mark Frost suggested we start a "train the trainer" program in which a trainee in a new process had to train others, too. This worked great, and we built consistency into our new processes.

"You are the only ones in the industry who consistently know what you're doing," our customers began saying to me.

I never tired of hearing this. But now that we were no longer a small shop that could manage by force of personality, we had to do more to beef up our culture. Zig Ziglar's training had been great for a while, especially his focus on building relationships and holding core values, but we needed to do more. We started a new teamwork initiative by hiring Andre Thornton, a pro baseball player who had eventually ended up with the Cleveland Indians.

After his pro ball career, Andre founded a consulting firm that helped people work in teams. He worked with our management team for over a year in the mid-1990s so we could create a culture in which people went from acting as individuals doing their own thing to acting as interdependent co-workers. Employees also learned how to be colleagues with our customers so our customer service managers could go beyond taking orders to having two-way conversations.

Andre did a great job, and he became close friends with us and others on our team. One day toward the end of Andre's consulting work with us, I realized change had really taken place. "You know what, Mike?" I said. "I think you and I are no longer the most important thing at the company. I think our culture is."

CHAPTER 39

Employee Assistance

JOHN

$$\left[-O - \underset{\underset{H}{|}}{\overset{\overset{CH_3}{|}}{C}} - \overset{\overset{O}{||}}{C} - O - \right]_n$$

We started ColorMatrix with profit in mind and with no philanthropic ideals. None.

When we located our first facility in Cleveland's inner city, we didn't do that because we wanted to be community oriented. We wanted cheap land and buildings. Knowing we would grow successfully, we wanted thousands of square feet of space. As a Rust Belt city, Cleveland offered downtown square footage that cost much less than space in places like Los Angeles, New York, and San Francisco. Downtown also offered cheaper land and facilities than suburbs because of Cleveland's many years of urban flight. We could lease space downtown for less than 50 percent of the suburban cost per square foot.

We figured we could deal with the issues that came with our low-cost location strategy when issues arose. And, whew, did they ever!

Statistically, Cleveland metropolitan area citizens were the urban poor. During the years we were growing our business, Cleveland lost nearly 40 percent of its manufacturing jobs, and saw its employment rate drop about 40 percent and its median family income by a third. By the end of the 1980s, one third of Clevelanders were living below the poverty line, often in single-mother households. Cleveland high schools graduated a tragically low percentage of students, and many students didn't come close to passing the most basic achievement tests required by the state.

Not only did Cleveland denizens not know how to work, many had no idea how to find the right clothes for work. A lack of winter coats, boots, hats, and mittens was a huge problem. *They don't know how to buy, set, or use an alarm clock, get themselves a bus pass, find childcare, open a bank account, or get themselves the right medicines,* I thought.

We contended with absenteeism, substance abuse, and educations that didn't go beyond the fifth grade. Workers often fell behind on their child or spousal support payments, and they occasionally had bench warrants against them—these are issued when someone doesn't respond to a subpoena for a legal infraction. On a few occasions, we watched as bail bondsmen escorted employees from the factory floor.

When employees needed bail money to get out of jail for minor offenses, made dumb financial decisions, or had paycheck garnishments that reduced their pay to nearly nothing, they raided their 401(k) accounts (if they had one) or came to us for help.

"I'm broke and I need money," they said.

We had no desire to deal with these entrenched societal problems, but the surprising thing was—and it's maybe the greatest surprise of our careers and lives—Mike and I grew to love offering people opportunities and then watching them grow in their careers. This was the most rewarding aspect of our years at ColorMatrix. We derived tremendous satisfaction from giving people a break, teaching them a work skill, and if they were willing to help themselves, helping them move quickly into positions with more responsibility.

We realized after a while that we needed to focus less on work skills and more on basic life skills. We started with creative employee assistance, talking with our employees preventively before they raided their 401(k) or made other poor financial decisions. When they came to me, I asked, "What do you need the money for?"

If they had a good reason and were good employees, Mike or I issued them a loan. We could have let our struggling employees live with the consequences of their bad personal financial decisions, but, first, we felt these were small amounts of money to us yet meant a lot to the employees. When people are shown love and empathy at difficult times in their lives, they often return the sentiment in the form of loyalty, which has a business benefit.

Second, we used these interactions as opportunities to build a relationship with the employee, namely through discussing a better way to handle their finances. We could send people to financial literacy classes all day long but the thing that made the most improvement was showing them, in the moment, how they could solve the issue at hand.

If an employee came back to us a second or third time over the same issue, we became more demanding and issued them a sterner rebuke. Mike and I willingly helped people and *supported* them in a time of need, but we didn't want to *enable* them by continuously issuing loans amid patterns of reckless behavior.

To people who don't run factories in inner cities, our

creative employee assistance programs seem strange. But we derived real satisfaction from giving people second chances and watching them flourish. Finding creativity, humor, and empathy inside ourselves energized us, as did helping our workers help themselves. In helping employees in need, I used a part of my brain and heart that totally surprised me and that (frankly) was under-utilized. That felt pretty great.

CHAPTER 40

Workforce Development

JOHN

In the late 1980s, we realized we needed a predictable, process-oriented hiring and retention plan to replace hope and good intentions for our unskilled but committed employees. Unfortunately, other than our made-up, "creative" employee assistance programs, we didn't have the slightest idea how to do this at scale.

One day we were explaining these workforce issues to a real estate developer. "You need to talk with David Roth, the head of Cleveland Works," he said.

In the 1980s, Ohio leaders formed Ohio Works as an offshoot of America Works, a national back-to-work training program based in Boston, Massachusetts. After a few years, deciding the program cost too much, the state stopped supporting Ohio Works. However, Cleveland leaders established Cleveland Works in 1994 to revive the notion of helping chronically unemployed people clean up their societal baggage and get back to work. Cleveland Works had a more enduring financial plan than Ohio Works did: it planned to raise local and regional funding to match federal funding from President Bill Clinton's new welfare-to-work initiative. The local and regional funding would be steadier than notoriously fickle state and federal funding.

From the outset, Cleveland Works had a great plan, making sure it was cost-efficient, at a few thousand dollars per person, while forging transformative impact. It targeted only heads of household on public assistance who had minimal job skills. Among other things, its staff provided 400 hours of instruction, including job readiness training that taught the responsibilities of being an employee and the expectations of an employer, helped trainees find work clothes and earn a GED, offered legal services, and ensured they had hygiene supplies such as soap, deodorant, hair brushes, and toothbrushes.

Cleveland Works also asked employers to partner with them by offering competitive wages and benefits and supporting the program over many months. That way, the program, the trainee, and the employer could work through problems. Personal and systemic change doesn't take place in a quarter or a year; it takes many years.

As soon as we met with David Roth, we knew Cleveland Works could play the training role we needed to hire and retain some of our employees. Working closely with David, we began an organized program of hiring for our factory-floor and office positions, with the idea of creating gateways for our employees—new careers rather than just jobs. In every case, we tried to put our employees in situations in which they'd develop a skill set and could further their education by taking classes. We paid above minimum wage and developed attractive health care benefits. We paid particularly close attention to women with children because they represented the largest category of need in the welfare-to-work initiative. Their health insurance needs differed from those of young, single men, and we had to address that difference.

Our first Cleveland Works hire was Linda, a single mother who worked in customer service and accounting. She was exactly the right hire.

"You know, she's great. I think this program is going to work for us," Mike said to David Roth.

Linda stayed with us for at least five years, a typical retention period for us through Cleveland Works. Our retention rate (the percent of new hires who stay at least one year) surpassed 80 percent for people hired through the program, while our retention when we used a temporary employment agency hovered around 50 percent. In our world, this represented a huge productivity increase and cost savings. We doubled down on our commitment to Cleveland Works and became one of the first businesses to donate money to the program. Mike also joined its board.

We found our quality manager, Jim, through the program. He had served in the military, so he understood responsibility but needed to build work skills. We hired him as a lab technician. He did a great job, and we transferred him to Texas to supervise quality control in the color lab. We also hired David, a native Liberian who had worked as a quality chemist on rubber plantations there. He and his wife came to the US as political refugees to flee the Liberian civil war. Even though David had a chemistry degree and knew how to work hard, he couldn't find a job. We ended up employing him in our lab as a product engineer.

Through Cleveland Works, we also hired a woman with children and a history of substance abuse. When she worked with us, she developed a sense of worth and responsibility. She held a technical position for years and then moved on to another company. We felt happy she had moved on to a bigger, better job and proud to have been a training ground for her new career.

Overall, we hired about 15 employees through Cleveland Works, and in most cases, they stayed with ColorMatrix until making their next career moves. We proudly helped them build resumes and transition into the workforce so they could move on to better things.

"I think we might have reached the point with this program where not only are we an attractive employer for people down on their luck," I said to Mike one day, "but also where they're attractive employees to us."

"It's a pretty great combination," he agreed.

Happily, our Cleveland Works relationship also turned into a philosophy about social responsibility. It helped us consistently fulfill our desire to support and mentor people and provide them with their first opportunity.

CHAPTER 41

Enablers?

JOHN

In business, you always have to think about what can go wrong. We had such admiration for joint ventures as our way to grow that we lost sight of the fact that partners sometimes become competitors. At other times, our partnering and mentoring philosophy fell flat.

First, our original partnership with Rosemar Industries and the three Chicago partners hadn't ended well.

Then our Brazilian partnership ended because we seriously disagreed with our co-owners in the venture about how to manage the business. Although we repurchased our equity and maintained our presence in Brazil, our partnership failed. (Fortunately, Dean Miller, who had scouted Brazil for us and was incredibly conscientious, continued to work with us in other places.)

Next, a South Korean distributor turned on us by deciding to collude with a South Korean colorant company to reverse-engineer and copy our colorant systems. The South Korean colorant company figured out the pigments, additives, and dispersion vehicles we used, copying our product and lowering the price. The Korean distributor picked up that product and dropped ours. Ben Chan had done a great job getting us into the South Korean market, but the unethical distributor ruined our efforts. At the same time, an unrelated company offered Ben a fantastic career opportunity.

"Ben decided to resign," Mike told me.

It was a loss to us. Mike and I bought back Ben's shares in ColorMatrix Asia, and while there were positive aspects about this deal, it nonetheless represented yet another failed partnership. We had endured risk and hardship to create opportunities for our partners in new industries and geographies, so the dissolutions of partnerships hurt our pride. We wondered too many times what we had done wrong.

Had we picked the wrong people?

Had we been too easy on people?

Should we be more litigious?

As we deconstructed each failed partnership, we realized that we had become "enablers." We too eagerly removed barriers for people and gave them opportunities like we had been given. We had to accept responsibility for the fact that we probably had made it too easy for some of our partners to succeed. We had to recognize that success may be better appreciated by people when some part of it is hard to come by.

"Mike, we need to stop *enabling* people! We need to *support* them, but not *enable* them."

In enabling, we made excuses for people who didn't need excuses. "They're going through a hard time, so let's let it slide," was the type of thing we said a lot. We took away the pain of overcoming problems by providing creative solutions to succeed, even though people didn't always ask us to do this. We had turned ourselves into enablers instead of supporters and mentors. We needed to start letting people sink or swim with their own capabilities and desires, not the capabilities and desires we had in mind for them. We needed to support, not enable, them.

We also had to accept an aspect of human nature: Some people will never be grateful for the opportunities they receive. They believe they are self-made. We needed to recognize this type of person earlier in our relationships and stop beating ourselves up when these people displayed ingratitude.

And we realized, too, that it is possible to outgrow people and companies. We were loyal and didn't want to simply dissolve a relationship with a good vendor, but we shouldn't let our loyalty stop us from limiting the scope of some vendor relationships. We gave each vendor the courtesy of openness and professionalism, explained that we were changing the relationship for a specific business purpose (not because we were unhappy), and gave them advance notice so the change wasn't overly detrimental.

As we changed, we began to shed our cycle of false hopes, disillusionment, and micromanagement. This transformed both of us as we went on our journey from $10 million to $100 million in revenue.

CHAPTER 42

City Hall

JOHN

$$\left[\begin{array}{c} \text{CH}_3 \ \text{O} \\ | \quad || \\ -\text{O}-\text{C}-\text{O}- \\ | \\ \text{H} \end{array}\right]_n$$

In the early 1990s, we were outgrowing our Cleveland facility and started to look for a new location. Very eager to remain in the city, we began meeting with politicians. We held our first meeting with then-Cleveland Mayor Michael White and his team at city hall.

"We have about 50 jobs," I said, directly and impatiently. "We're a good employer. Our plan is to leave the city if you don't give us $250,000 to stay."

I had no desire to engage in small talk or beat around the bush. I wanted what I wanted. Evidently, that was a problem.

"No dice. Have a nice day," Mayor White retorted, pretty much exactly like that, adding a few words to explain that the city didn't provide business retention grants, so we weren't going to get anywhere with his administration. End of conversation.

I did go away from the meeting thinking, *This mayor is good.* He was imposing, confident, and didn't pull his punches. He had 80 lawyers, 30 unions and 10,000 employees to manage, so I shouldn't have been surprised.

"Well, that didn't go so well," Mike said as we walked to the parking garage.

"Nope," I said. "I guess issuing ultimatums isn't the way to go."

We regrouped and did our homework on company retention mechanisms the city found palatable, discovering that it did use tax abatements. Preparation completed, we requested another meeting. We offered our thoughts and analysis on a proposed tax abatement plan, and this meeting went much better.

Mayor White's team, along with Mike, and I crunched numbers for a ten-year inventory and property tax abatement plan. We came up with a scenario that saved us real money and was feasible for the city.

"How long does it take to package this proposal and push it through the approval process with city council?" I asked.

The mayor seemed to appreciate that for businesses, time is money, because he responded firmly. "I am authorized to offer this," he said. He explained that our plan didn't subtract from the tax base because we would still pay our current taxes; we just wouldn't pay taxes on increased levels of inventory and new property. The city required us to show that we could create at least ten jobs, which would substantially outweigh the benefit of foregone property tax revenue because the city would get two percent of payroll. He emphasized in closing that we had a good plan in front of us, and we should consider it approved.

I was awestruck and chastened. "Once we spoke his language and gave him tools and terms within his bailiwick, he moved lightning fast," I told our CFO back at the plant. "I learned a lot about how to do business with the city today."

We worked with Mayor White's administration numerous times and found his focus on job creation to be right on target. We created at least 50 jobs, in contrast to the ten for which the mayor had asked—one small win for Cleveland, which was losing manufacturing jobs to low-cost labor in Asia and sometimes to better deals in the Cleveland suburbs. At conferences and events, the mayor held up ColorMatrix as an example of smart and hard-won job creation.

CHAPTER 43

Bye, Cleveland

JOHN

During Mayor White's time in office, we moved into a new facility on Chester Avenue and stayed there for ten years. At almost 100,000 square feet, the Chester plant was large enough for us and our projected growth, but its layout was wrong. Our building had three floors and this vertical layout was not consistent with lean manufacturing practices. For our operation to be efficient, we needed to find a one-floor location.

Although Cleveland has plenty of dilapidated old buildings, the inventory of structures that would suit our needs was not promising. Yet we badly wanted to stay in the city. We had by this time been placed on the list of the highest-growth private companies in America's inner cities. We had risen in the ranks over the years, eventually making it as high as 37th on the *Inc.* 100 Inner City Company list for our size and growth rate.

In one of its introductions to the annual ranking, *Inc.* wrote:

Because of their locations, the companies honored here sometimes find life a little more challenging than many other businesses do. But that has only made them more creative. On the flip side, the CEOs who grew up in these inner-city neighborhoods often find their success—and their consequent ability to give back to their communities—more than usually gratifying. Great companies are born in garages and office parks and basements and incubators. And thanks to factors ranging from diverse workforces to innovative investment programs, more and more are born on city streets.

This captured our sentiment. We loved our location in Cleveland and were willing to go to great lengths to find the right building so we could stay there.

Jane Campbell served as mayor after Mike White. We set up a meeting with her team. We had learned a lot from working with Mayor White's administration, and we felt well-versed in how to approach city hall. Of course, a new administration always brings a different way of operating, but Mike and I underestimated the extent to which things would change.

We met with Mayor Campbell's economic development director, Chris Warren, a sharp guy who grasped our needs immediately. He sent us to see Mayor Campbell. That's when things took a turn for the worse.

She didn't ask good questions and quickly shuffled us along to someone who drove us around to look at buildings. This guy started showing us five-story buildings served by a single elevator.

"This isn't working," I said. "So far not one building has met a single one of our top three requirements."

Mike and I took matters into our own hands. We found a building we thought might work: an old manufacturing building in the heart of Midtown that the city had acquired in 1991. By 2001, when we found it, the place looked like it had been sitting around for a thousand years. It was abandoned, had boarded up windows and a collapsing roof, and showed scars where scavengers had ripped away the copper and aluminum. When we went inside, though, it didn't look as bad because the city had rehabilitated half of it. And we needed only the ground floor.

We went back to the mayor.

"That building could work," I said.

Her stream-of-consciousness reply, as I recall, went something like this . . . *oh, you can't have that building . . . we park the city's school buses in the parking lot there . . . if you took that parking lot, I wouldn't have any place to park the school buses.*

I didn't have enough experience to know whether White was really good or Campbell was really bad, but I am guessing that her response was typical among her mayoral peers. Michael Porter, a Harvard Business School professor who runs a national program called the Initiative for Competitive Inner Cities, once asked his research team to survey companies that had left inner cities. Porter's team reported in *Inc.* magazine that "the number one reason by far, like five times over No. 2, is that they couldn't expand in the time frame they required," he said.

That was our problem with the new Cleveland regime—slowness and unresponsiveness. But I still held out a glimmer of hope. I had learned about the state of Ohio's program for existing Ohio companies that build new facilities. For these companies, the state offered loans at attractive rates—one percent interest for the first three years and three percent interest after that.

Our CFO and I went back to Mayor Campbell. "Do you have any interest in partnering on this?" I asked. "If you got a real estate developer to build a facility at those terms, we would commit to a long-term lease."

She stared at us as if to say, "Now, how would you get that done?" followed by another stream-of-consciousness reply, something along the lines of *we haven't done this . . . it's new to us . . .*

"I'm done," I said. "There is no way her administration will ever want to work with us."

Mike and I had loved supporting the city and being supported in return, but we had an urgent need to expand. In Berea, fifteen miles west of Cleveland, we found an empty building owned by a developer who agreed to make leasehold improvements for us. The mayor of Berea welcomed us and made relocating attractive by refunding a portion of the city's payroll tax. We needed cost concessions like this to compete with the Chinese and other foreign governments, which were throwing piles of money at their manufacturers, enabling them to grow. We weren't going to win on labor costs. And while we competed with China (and others) largely with our value-added solutions, we also had to manage operating costs very tightly to drive the efficiencies that made us competitive.

We pulled the trigger, and in 2003, we struck a five-year lease agreement with the developer and Berea. We moved in shortly afterward. I bought a glass-topped, art deco wooden table for my new office, decorated the walls (pictures of my wife; my boat; and me playing pit crew at a Las Vegas speedway; a pencil etching of the names of three friends listed on the Vietnam memorial; and a print of our company logo, a tiger), and was happy with my new office. But every day I walked into it, I missed Cleveland. We had been so proud of being an inner-city company and creating jobs.

CHAPTER 44

Dark Cloud

MIKE

ColorMatrix Europe had become very capable at quickly capitalizing on each new opportunity, serving as a better partner than we ever could have imagined ten years earlier when Bill came into my office looking for a business reason to get to the UK. Around 2003, our initial ten-year agreement with them was due to expire. We owned the TripleA scavenger and Amosorb licenses, and we also owned the know-how, which we licensed to them. That said, the Europeans had also developed their own in-house know-how such that ours was no longer a huge asset.

They held goals similar to ours, and they had reasonable requests in the agreement renegotiation. But we found one of their points difficult to swallow. They wanted the new joint venture agreement to contain a provision for a sale of their ColorMatrix Europe business that would generate cash for them.

"They've worked hard, and now they want to cash out," I told John. "But I want them to be co-owners for a lot longer because there's so much more opportunity for all of us to capture."

I probed Bill on why his team desired liquidity. He repeated that they considered cash to be increasingly important. This also held true for John and me, but for us, timing was more the issue. We wanted to wait longer to cash out than did our European partners.

"They say our renewed agreement has to have a liquidity provision," I told John. "For them, it's a non-negotiable term."

This was a problem because we needed Bill, Dave, and Mark. They had turned Europe into a backbone of profitability and growth for ColorMatrix. At an intellectual level, we understood their desire, but in our hearts, we wanted them to keep growing. In the end, we had no choice but to include the provision. We completed the agreement renewal, which stated that if a company didn't acquire ColorMatrix overall, then John and I would be required to buy them out of ColorMatrix Europe.

Partly because of this situation, we were of two minds. On the one hand, we felt great. It seemed like the world was our oyster:

- We had our colorant systems, which were customized solutions for customers.
- We provided training and customer support, which included technical support from centers in the US and Europe.
- We owned rights to proprietary additives like the TripleA scavenger and Amosorb.
- We had finally become an international chemicals company. We had locations on four continents and

sold our colorant solutions into every continent on the globe.

- We counted some of the biggest corporate names as customers or end users—Coca-Cola, Pepsi, Heineken, Anheuser-Busch, J.M. Smucker Co., Rubbermaid, Royal Appliance, Mitsubishi, Colgate-Palmolive, and many other huge companies.

- We also supplied color to 70 percent of PVC pipe customers in North America, companies like Cantex and Carlon.

- From a knowledge standpoint, we had a lock on the largest and fastest-growing plastics markets: consumer packaged products (PET), building and construction products (PVC), and plastic consumer products (traditional injection-molded plastics).

- And liquid colorants were a growing area, having reached 5-10 percent of the plastics industry, up from about 1 percent when we had started in the early 1980s.

On the other hand, the liquidity requirement for the European team presented a dark cloud over John and me. It unsettled us and changed how we thought about our roles in our global business. I sat at my antique desk and stared out the window. *What the heck are we going to do?* I wondered.

PART III

Selling

CHAPTER 45

Leveraged Recap

JOHN

In 1996 when I was 50 years old, I had a quadruple bypass. My heart condition and surgery had helped me make changes over the years. I ate more healthily, sold my boats, and while I continued to work hard, I stepped back a bit from the constant stress of selling and solving problems. I liked this change—being more strategic, making fewer sales calls, and relinquishing the responsibility of making most of our hiring decisions. Mike also had pulled up a level, driven by his desire to enable the business to grow more quickly and flexibly.

I was having fun with this new role, and we were growing like gangbusters, reaching about $100 million in annual revenue. "This company can do much more," I said. I didn't want to sell the business.

"It can," Mike agreed, "but buying out Bill, David, and Mark is going to take a heap of cash."

The European deal term threw *me* for a loop, too. Technically, we had enough cash. But using the cash and a lot of bank debt to buy out our European partners would cause enormous financial stress. Neither Mike nor I wanted that stress in our lives. "Maybe it's time to take on investors. We could sell a stake in the company," I said.

The equity-investor path was one we thought we'd never take, but we had changed. After talking with our accounting firm, bank, and others, we figured out that selling a minority equity stake to investors so we could maintain a controlling interest wouldn't fly.

"If an investor is going to put a bunch of money into your company,"—we were thinking about raising over $50 million—"they're going to want a controlling stake," our advisors told us.

Investors at that amount of capital require the authority to make decisions, which meant we were going to have to find an investor to buy over 50 percent of our business. We didn't want to sell 100 percent because we wanted to remain actively involved. We needed a recapitalization of Color-Matrix that would accomplish all our goals. We wanted to:

- Raise cash to buy out the Europeans and grow the business,
- Monetize some of our own equity stake,
- Continue to own a large portion of the company (albeit not a majority), and
- Keep working at ColorMatrix.

We needed to find buyers who wanted us to remain active with the company rather than kick us to the curb. We wanted an experienced firm to do the transaction, and we wanted to avoid seller's remorse. Research shows that half of owners who sell their companies feel like they left money on the table. The sellers might not have wanted to sell in the first place, or perhaps they set the wrong sale price or were taken advantage of by the buyers.

"We could decide not to sell the business," I said to Mike. I was so wary of experiencing seller's remorse.

"That's what we're doing, in a way," he pointed out. "Because we're not selling it, we're recapping it."

Rather than selling, we were weaning ourselves from ColorMatrix. We were determined to get a fair price. And we weren't naïve sellers who would let a seasoned buyer take advantage of us.

CHAPTER 46

I-Bankers

JOHN

"You need to find an investment banker for your recap," our accountant told Mike. "They do deals all day long and know how to get you a good price."

The bankers could write our offering memorandum, conduct the auction that created a competition for the deal, and create the right go-forward financial structure. We had avoided working with investment bankers nearly a decade earlier, in 1997, when an unsolicited bid had come in for our company. Instead we had asked Ernst & Young to put together a basic booklet that functioned as an ad hoc offering memorandum. Only one buyer had been involved, and when our half-hearted efforts to respond to their bid failed to yield a fair price, we happily terminated the deal.

"It's different now," Mike said as we talked about our disappointments with that experience. "We know we want to sell—we're not just responding to a bid—so we should use an investment bank."

We met with the sell-side teams at a handful of investment banks and found that bankers and their firms were as different as day and night. After the third or fourth meeting, we decided to work with Grace Matthews in Milwaukee, Wisconsin, co-founded by Doug Mittman and John Beagle, two chemical engineers with MBAs. A finance and accounting expert, Doug was outspoken, opinionated, and matter of fact. He didn't pull his punches. John was strategic, sales-oriented, and incredibly pleasant, a good yin to Doug's yang. Their company had a terrific reputation for mergers and acquisitions in the specialty chemicals industry and offered all the best of a regional investment bank. Doug and John had a down-to-earth style, showed high interest in our company, knew our industry well, and focused on one outcome: a successful recap.

"One of the things that impresses us most about Color-Matrix is the partnership between you two," one of them said. "In the past, we've been brought in to represent a bunch of companies where the partners were at loggerheads with each other."

"It's amazing you have worked together for over 30 years," the other said. (If you included our five years working together at Cincinnati Milacron, this was true.)

"We've never really had a substantial disagreement," I said.

Our partnership wasn't perfect. I didn't tell the investment bankers about the couple of times we annoyed each other and needed to walk away to hide our frustration. But staying together when most partnerships failed boiled down to one thing: respect for one another. My hot temper aside, we never second-guessed each other, and we always kept the business moving forward.

CHAPTER 47

How Big Companies Think

JOHN

Before we signed on with Grace Matthews, Mike wanted to add someone to our team. "What do you think of the idea of adding Polymer TransAction to our team on this transaction?" Mike asked John and Doug.

Bill Ridenour, the head of Polymer TransAction Advisors, had called on us for years, eager to represent us in a transaction. Mike had always liked Bill and wanted to get him on our team because he had a deep understanding of the plastics industry.

We all agreed that Bill should be a special advisor to Grace Matthews in the transaction, so our transaction team was set, and John and Doug kicked off the selling process. We met at our offices in Berea.

"If you want someone with deep pockets who'll pay a premium, you've got to be global," Doug said.

"We are global," I responded. "We have operations in China, South America . . . "

He stopped me short.

"John, you're international, which is great," I recall him

saying. "But you're not global. Each of your locations is its own independent entity, and each one has its own structure and relationship to the US headquarters."

"Sure," I shot back. "Hong Kong is a distributorship because that's always our first step into foreign markets. The UK is a full licensee with joint ownership because they're farther along, and so they reached step two of our joint venture process."

I had wanted to explain how well we had managed our entries into various markets but the Grace Matthews guys showed that that they didn't care about that because they looked at the world from the viewpoint of big-company buyers. That was their job—to know what big-company buyers wanted.

"Your international locations do business under the ColorMatrix name," he said, "but you don't operate as one company. You have pocketed entrepreneurship with an international presence."

"You say that like it's a bad thing," I said, wondering how being international and entrepreneurial could be bad.

"You need to become one global, coordinated company," Doug continued, saying his firm would set out this strategy in our offering memorandum.

His insight hurt our pride. The independence we offered our joint venture partners had constituted an inviolable operating principle for years.

"We have completely forgotten how big companies think," Mike concluded. "John and Doug have sold about forty companies in our space (specialty chemicals and additives), and they know what's going to work for big companies."

In our subsequent meetings with Doug and John, we all worked to design our strategy so that big companies could plug ColorMatrix into their global operations. If we had a cookie-cutter approach of doing things at each location around the globe, we would make multinationals much more comfortable.

Under their guidance, we positioned each of our primary locations in the US, Europe, China, and Brazil as a center of excellence for a specific capability. The UK became our research and development and our global packaging (PET) industry center of excellence, and the US became a center of excellence for developing new equipment (such as our metering devices) and industrial extrusion (PVC) processes.

We also improved our IT systems. Mike and I always found IT expenditures to be painful. Every time we analyzed the economics of IT projects compared to investments in machinery, new products, people, and partnerships, the return on investment hardly made us jump up and down with excitement. Avoiding the 1990s and early 2000s allure of investing in expensive IT trends hadn't seemed to hurt us, but Bill, David, and Mark in Europe had long implored us to put more money into our systems.

"New systems will increase European sales at least five percent," they had told us a few times over the years.

If true, such investment admittedly did make good economic sense. "Might be true," I had responded each time, "but our style is to pick up the phone and visit a customer, so let's stick with that." Silence on the other end of the phone was the usual response, likely the sound of people pulling out their hair.

Now our bankers were saying to us, "You have got to

invest in IT." They said it would help create that cookie-cutter operation that would increase the price we fetched for the business.

"We need to maximize the price of the business," Mike reasoned. "That's as good a return on investment as it gets."

So, we followed their advice and invested in systems.

CHAPTER 48

Sellers' Anxiety

JOHN

Next on our emotional hit parade was the fun experience of seller's anxiety.

"I'm constantly afraid this transaction is going to fall apart," I said to Mike when we were knee-deep in the selling process. My anxiety was based on the daily, relentless grind of what we had to do for the recap transaction—it took tremendous time, and when you are selling a business, there are more opportunities for things to go wrong than right. "If this deal dies, we have serious issues," I said. "We need to get this thing done as quickly as possible."

Topping the list of those issues was the high fees we were paying Doug and John. We couldn't recoup those fees if the deal failed. Although we would pay a success fee only upon consummation of a transaction, we were also paying them a retainer fee.

Second on the list of issues: We were about to spend a year (the length of time a recap transaction typically takes) improving our company for sale rather than ongoing operations. We would take our eye off the ball, operationally, for an extended period. Dave McBride, John Standish, Gerry Corrigan, and others were running the business, but we needed their time and energy spent on this transaction, as well. The divided focus meant we ought to plan on working extra hard and lower company performance for a while.

The third issue causing us anxiety was, if the transaction failed, our employees would suddenly know Mike and I had tried to sell our stake in the business.

"They'll think we don't care about the business anymore," I said to our transaction team when I explained why I considered confidentiality of this transaction to be so important.

Money down the drain, subpar business performance, and low morale constituted our trio of transaction-failure nightmares. If the transaction failed, we faced a similar experience as publicly held companies that fail to complete a sale—a decline in the seller's stock price to pre-transaction-discussion levels or lower.

To counteract this risk—and ensure a buyer is really motivated even in the face of deal-related problems that inevitably arise—some sellers write a break-up fee into an agreement. The buyer has to pay the seller a fee if they break off the transaction during due diligence. It partially compensates the seller for that negative stock-price effect. But Doug and John thought breakup fees offered an "easy out" to buyers, which they didn't want to offer.

"Nerve-racking" is a good way to describe the year-long process in which Doug and John collected information from our management team, created an offering memorandum, generated interest from buyers, confirmed interest from a select few, and then shepherded us through due diligence with the company that presented the best letter of intent to do the recap.

This last step—exclusive due diligence during which we negotiated with one buyer *who had all the power*—was the worst. It seemed like the buyer could use any information or event that might have an adverse effect on the value of ColorMatrix as reason to discount the sale price.

For instance, in our offering memorandum, we included projections for revenue and EBITDA (earnings before interest, taxes, depreciation, and amortization; a measure of profitability). If we didn't hit or surpass the projections, the buyer could use the shortfall to decrease the price. And yet we had to take our eye off growing revenues and EBITDA in order to conduct the all-consuming recapitalization transaction. We had to rely on Dave, the Europeans, and others to keep up our sales and profits.

We figured that a large specialty chemicals company would pay the most for our company because they would get market share gains and cost savings from integrating our products into theirs. But private equity investors bid on us because leveraged recaps like ours were their bread and butter. They knew how to get debt financing, put together a syndicate of lenders, work with business owners, and quickly improve a company for sale at a higher price.

We eventually agreed to move into exclusive due diligence with Audax, a private equity firm out of Boston, Massachusetts. They seemed most likely to put together the right financing and ownership package.

"Plus, John and I like them," Mike told Doug, our investment banker.

Our bankers told us the industry respected Audax confirmed that they could put together the right financing package. But none of us could have predicted the trajectory of the US economy. In 2006, it showed signs of weakness, led by the accumulating troubles of the housing and banking sectors. The booming housing market turned to bust by late 2006, home sales fell, and economists talked about a housing bubble.

You don't want to hear the word "bubble" when you are on the verge of selling your business. It implies "bursting," which implies impending doom for buyers who overpay. People also threw around the phrase "liquidity crunch" a lot—another term you don't want to hear when your business is amid a major debt-financing transaction.

Every time he listened to the news, Mike became extremely agitated.

"John, there's a real risk Audax won't be able to secure bank financing," he said.

As our strategist, Mike excelled at collecting information and making sense of it, and he didn't like what he saw on the horizon. He hated the risks he saw in the economy, and it showed.

"Mike, are you sleeping these days?" I asked him.

"Not much," he said.

"You look like you're losing weight, too," I said.

"Yup."

His states of mind and health concerned me, but I couldn't do much to help.

CHAPTER 49

Panic Attack

JOHN

W̲e were on the verge of completing a key step in the transaction when everything related to the transaction suddenly came to a standstill. I didn't know why.

They want to decrease the price, I thought.

They think there's going to be a meltdown in the economy.

They can't get financing.

As it turned out, the reason for the holdup had a mundane and easily resolvable root cause—in our due diligence materials, we hadn't included the certificate of approval from a tiny Eastern European country to sell our products there.

Audax interacted with us well throughout our due diligence process. They even allocated a stock option pool to Mike and me so we would have additional upside post-transaction. We met with one of Audax's partners, Keith Palumbo, about the pool. He was down-to-earth, someone you wanted to be around, and really bright. We explained to him what we wanted to do.

"John and I are interested in reallocating some of our

stock options to some employees," Mike said. "Do you have any issues with this?"

We had always wanted to be the only employee-owners of ColorMatrix equity—we felt that we should incur the financial risk (and upside) for the company. Also, attracting great people to ColorMatrix had never required us to issue options. Our opportunistic, chemical and additive company differed from Silicon Valley companies, which developed breakthrough technologies and new markets and therefore often needed to offer stock options to recruit and retain top people. Our employees valued salary and cash bonuses more than illiquid equity. We did, however, want some employees to benefit from the new ownership structure, and we gave up some of our own stock option pool to do that. We talked with them and confirmed they would appreciate our stock option reallocation plan, and fortunately, Keith approved its general outlines.

Then one day, when none of the news on the economy or the transaction was good and, indeed, some of it was bad, I noticed that Mike looked really uncomfortable.

"Are you sweating?" I asked him.

"Yeah," he said, "I sure am. You know, John, there's a good possibility this transaction could go south."

Mike was having a panic attack. Concerned about his health, I just listened. He said the facts pointed to a serious possibility of a failed transaction. We got John and Doug on the phone and talked through our fears.

They responded with an exactly right, matter-of-fact, informed tone. Matters that we considered to be a hurricane they considered to be a gentle breeze. We realized that owners like us sell a business once, maybe twice, in a lifetime, so everything is new, and we don't recognize the pattern of a deal. But the bankers have seen it all. They recognize patterns across many transactions and know which problems are serious and which ones aren't. The Grace Matthews guys calmed Mike and me down.

CHAPTER 50

String of Successes

JOHN

A round ten months into the leveraged recap process, Geoff Rehnert and Mark Wolpow, the co-CEOs of Audax, visited us. This meeting was important because we had to like them, and they had to like us for our recap to be completed. Bright and people-oriented, Geoff always made a point of meeting business owners and hearing their stories. He wanted to get a sense of the heritage and heartbeat of businesses before buying them. Mark, a disarmingly direct, steel-blue-eyed guy, complemented Geoff nicely.

The visit went well, and on May 24, 2006, Geoff, Mark and the Audax team acquired ColorMatrix for $175 million, which represented a healthy revenue and earnings multiple in any environment, never mind the then-deteriorating economic conditions. We held a company-wide meeting to explain that we had recapitalized ColorMatrix to take advantage of growth opportunities.

"Mike and I are still involved with the business," I said. "We're co-chairmen, and we'll now have deeper pockets so we can grow faster."

ColorMatrix employees took the news in stride. A number of employees who received deferred compensation or stock options likely would do well when Audax decided to sell the business, and our European partners were happy to be bought out. Mike and I went to Morton's Steakhouse to join our management team, bankers, European co-owners, and new owners for a celebration. Sitting there, I soaked up Mike's and my new situation in life. Our new owners knew how to manage and lead businesses like ColorMatrix; we had capitalized ColorMatrix for new growth; and our employees stood to do well, financially and professionally.

"Wow, somehow we have cobbled together a string of successes over the past 25 years, huh?" I said to Mike.

A glass of wine or two can make a person nostalgic. I thought about me as the small-town guy and Mike, the salesman, selling like crazy and solving customer problems for a quarter of a century, forging joint ventures because we didn't have money to start new businesses from scratch, and now, we were wealthy.

"I never ever imagined we would create a business that someone would value at nearly $200 million, Mike."

"We had some great mentors on the way," he said. "You know, they probably believed in us more than we believed in ourselves."

Many people had generated this success—employees, vendors, partners, mentors, and our families—by believing in us. And we had forged a terrific partnership with each other. Not everything we had done had succeeded, but we had never blamed each other, wallowed in indecision, or had a serious disagreement. I had come to love Mike like a brother, even if his personality differed significantly from mine. Mike may have preferred horseback riding with his wife and daughters to the speed-boat racing and skeet shooting with buddies that I enjoyed, but I was grateful that my business partner had stuck by me through the years.

A week after the transaction, I found in my day planner the list of documents the federal authorities had taken from us when they investigated us in the mid-1980s. I had always kept the list near me because I lived in terror of a repeat experience. For 25 years, I had been waiting for us to be falsely accused again, and the piece of paper had served as my security blanket. I always imagined pulling it out, gathering up the documents on the list, providing them to the authorities, and being cleared of whatever the false accusations might be.

I unfolded the paper, tore it up, and threw it into the waste basket.

CHAPTER 51

Growth Drivers

MIKE

With the deal completed, I could step back from the business yet remain involved, a perfect situation. Years earlier, John and I had recruited Gerry Corrigan to help us turn our scrap material into cash. He had done such a bang-up job that we had made him our chief operating officer. Audax went further, promoting him to chief executive officer.

Meanwhile, John and I co-chaired the ColorMatrix board, which entailed attending weekly conference calls and periodic in-person meetings. We dealt with a few Audax guys, including Keith Palumbo and Oliver Ewald, an Audax partner from Germany who did a great job structuring information for good decision-making.

A company moves forward because people make good decisions, and Oliver brought this mindset to ColorMatrix. I enjoyed watching his impatience grow on the occasions when someone didn't operate in that same fact-finding and decision-making mode because I had a similar tendency as him. Steve Loose, another Audax guy, had a background in investing, operations, and consulting, and he constantly pushed for growth and opportunity.

These three men, Keith, Ollie, and Steve, constituted the right combination for ColorMatrix. They wanted to invest for growth, which was a change for me because I had always conserved cash. ColorMatrix needed the Audax growth approach, but as co-chairman, I needed to adapt and catch up. The private equity guys played the game of trying to increase the value of ColorMatrix quickly so they could "sell high." They knew that plastics companies didn't garner high revenue or profit multiples, and neither did the vast majority of colorant companies, but specialty chemical companies did. Keith, Ollie, and Steve wanted to ensure that we positioned ColorMatrix squarely as a global specialty chemicals company.

They watched ColorMatrix growth drivers religiously and dialed into the details of each revenue stream with the precision of engineers. They knew exactly how long it took to convert a prospect into a paying customer, and they developed Gantt charts that broke down the mechanics and economics of the ColorMatrix sales pipeline. This reverse engineering of the factors that drove our business interested, entertained, and impressed us.

"The things we've treated as intuition or idiosyncrasy, they treat like science," John observed.

With each analysis they performed, they found a new way to finely tune a ColorMatrix growth driver. We were amazed.

We learned a ton by watching Audax, but it wasn't all rosy. The financial crisis became a source of stress. ColorMatrix was doing well, but the Audax team thought we needed to take preventive action. They wanted ColorMatrix to cut costs globally, to conserve cash in the plunging economy. They assigned acting CEO John Gelp the task of managing cash flow among our European, South American, and Asian operations. John also dealt with a scared and skittish bank syndicate. He spent hours each week managing the bank covenants under which ColorMatrix operated and led the effort to decrease costs so we wouldn't violate the covenants. He laid off employees, reduced our purchases, extended our working capital, and put together contingency plans. These ranged from mild recession-style scenarios to hell-in-a-hand-basket scenarios. Our European team wasn't seeing the gathering gloom we were seeing because the US entered the financial crisis before Europe did. As a result, having to do layoffs displeased them.

Another thing that John and I didn't enjoy was being out of the driver's seat for key relationships. We had built up many vendor relationships over 25 years, and we considered some of them very special. I would have loved for Color-Matrix to continue these relationships as a reward to our vendors for past service. But we didn't own the company anymore, so we couldn't own what happened to those relationships. We influenced some, but Audax replaced many others with its own ecosystem of vendors. I understood these actions, but John and I didn't enjoy relinquishing our roles in key relationships.

CHAPTER 52

A Global Enterprise

MIKE

One day, BP contacted us about the possibility of selling us its entire oxygen scavenger patent portfolio. This fit perfectly with Audax's strategy of adding proprietary technologies that enabled ColorMatrix to serve more additives needs for customers. Audax wanted to increase our "stickiness" with customers because that would generate the revenue and earnings growth to command higher sale multiples whenever Audax decided to sell. We owned or exclusively licensed proprietary products, such as our colorant formulations, our TripleA scavenger, and our Amosorb technologies. Audax wanted more.

"We're a specialty chemical company masquerading as a plastics colorants company," I said to John after one board meeting when we saw the full vision Audax had for our transformation to a specialty chemicals company. I enjoyed seeing the plan unfold.

I went to meet with BP, and they had two points. First, they had a directive to focus on their core business and get rid of non-core assets. Second, our product development efforts and theirs overlapped in the area of oxygen scavenging. They wanted to sell us their oxygen scavenger patent portfolio.

After some discussion, I asked, "What's the price tag on this?"

We were already paying a lot to BP in royalties on its patents. If we bought the technology outright, we could stop paying the royalty fees. They gave us a number. Back at Audax, Ollie liked the idea of acquiring BP's patent portfolio, but did not like the price they gave. We negotiated down the price to the point that it became a good deal for both sides, but then things stalled because BP didn't know which person in its bureaucracy should put his or her signature on the deal. The deal made sense for both sides, but the BP executives didn't want to stick out their necks.

I kept thinking, *that's the big-company way of doing things, and I have to say, I don't miss that way of operating.*

I placed a few phone calls to BP and after going in circles for a while asked, "What will it take to get a signature on this?"

Finally, they made a decision. We closed on the patents in 2008, and Amosorb soon grew to be a substantial global business for us. Audax proved to be right in its belief that owning technologies versus licensing gave us a shot at growing even faster. With enough cash to purchase product lines, Audax made this strategy work!

Audax also decided to increase our footprint in China, considering the country had over a billion citizens and a rapidly rising consumer class. In China, we had stalled at Step One of our original geographic market entry strategy (i.e., export first) and never reached Step Two (i.e., setting up manufacturing). For years, we had exported colorant systems from the US to Hong Kong, where we warehoused them. Hong Kong then supplied our products to a converter in Wan Chai, China, a city filled with massive industrial complexes and that can only be described as a feat of modern Chinese economic policy. In Wan Chai, individual operations don't even have names. They're not so much companies as government entities established to produce goods for export so China's masses can be put to work.

Audax knew China represented enormous opportunity. Our investors made ColorMatrix UK the support center for China and tasked Bill Ravenna with growing our presence in China by adding manufacturing capability there. He opened a plant in Suzhou, an hour or so from Shanghai. Like Wan Chai, Suzhou consisted of industrial complexes as far as the eye could see. ColorMatrix sales in China grew dramatically.

Further, under Audax leadership, we made acquisitions. Audax charged me with figuring out good targets. We became interested in a family-owned company called Dosicolor, a leading South and Central America supplier of liquid colorants. If we acquired them, we'd be the largest liquid colorant company in Latin America. The population of its three primary markets—Mexico, Argentina, and Brazil—totaled 350 million people, about the same as the US population. Ollie and I traveled to Argentina and convinced the Dosicolor owners that an acquisition made sense.

After this, we made more acquisitions. Steve Loose led the acquisition of Colorant Chromatics, a Finnish company focused on the wire and cable market. Wire and cable casings are colored according to the function of their wire and are made from a specialty plastic that's heat stable at very high temperatures. It's flame-resistant and doesn't emit smoke so it can be safely used in high-heat places such as car engines. A handful of companies across the globe made colorants for this specialty plastic, and Colorant Chromatics was one of them. Because of its niche, it generated high margins. (We usually avoided solid color concentrate because it was lower margin.) I worked with Steve to make the acquisition, which added to our earnings and gave us a new specialty-product line.

More acquisitions followed. For years, I had held casual, exploratory conversations about a "potential business combination" with Bob Bradley and Robbie Droman, co-owners of Gayson Silicone Dispersions near Akron. Their company made silicone colorants and additives for rubber. Keith Palumbo, who had become our primary Audax point person, worked with us to turn the conversations into a transaction. In April 2011, we acquired Gayson, the final piece of Audax's strategy to make us a global chemical and additives company. We had 14 locations around the world, including Ohio (2), South Carolina (which manufactured our dispersion pumps), Texas, Connecticut (through the Finland acquisition), Brazil, Argentina, Mexico, the UK, the Netherlands, Finland, Hong Kong, and China (2).

We had wholesale transformed into a global enterprise. When we started in the early 1980s, I scratched my head trying to figure out how we could reach $69,000 in revenue, and now I co-chaired and held equity in a company that generated $175 million in annual revenue and 15 percent top-line growth.

John and Doug at Grace Matthews had told us that whoever acquired our company would move it away from being an "international presence and pocketed entrepreneurship" and toward being a fully global specialty chemical and additives business.

"I think we've made that change," I said to John at our plant in Berea.

CHAPTER 53

Ready to Sell

MIKE

Private equity firms need to generate a return on investment in a roughly six-year window, which means Audax
planned to sell ColorMatrix a handful of years after acquiring it. Near the four-year anniversary of owning us, Keith
said Audax was ready to sell, and he planned to use Baird as
the investment bank for the transaction. Baird checked most
of the important boxes: It was established, had an international presence and many connections with major companies around the globe, and a strong process for selling companies. It knew well the process of generating interest from
buyers, creating competition for the deal, driving buyers to
sign letters of intent, seeing buyers and sellers through the
due diligence process, and closing the deal.

"But Grace Matthews was so great for us," I said to John.
"I'd like to see if we can get them involved in this."

John and I wanted to make sure that as minority owners,
we had someone representing our interests. Audax bought
and sold companies constantly and had supplied Baird with

numerous deals (and, therefore, cash), but we hadn't. Contractually, Baird, which was a great firm, worked for Audax.

We thought, *Who is representing us?*

Grace Matthews' representation of us in the first transaction had meant a lot to us. We explained our desires to Keith, and convinced him that Doug and John knew Color-Matrix, specialty chemicals, and us, and so would make a good additional banker in the deal.

"Okay, how about we use two investment banks?" he suggested. "We'll go with both Baird and Grace Matthews."

His concession made us happy. Then again, Keith held firm on a different matter. Because neither John nor I would be involved with ColorMatrix after its sale—our remaining equity stake would be bought out by the buyer—Audax wanted to remove us fully from the sale process. It needed to avoid a situation in which buyers could say, "If these guys, the co-founders and co-chairmen, aren't with the business, then the business doesn't have value."

Having been through our own experience of trying to avoid every item that could reduce the price of our business in the recap four years prior, we understood his concerns. John and I would be completely sidelined during the deal. The ColorMatrix management team would do the work, incentivized in part by a combination of straight stock ownership and a stock option plan that vested upon a sale of the entire company.

The bankers sent out the offering memos, and within a few weeks, Grace Matthews and Baird heard back from companies interested in proceeding to due diligence. Doug winnowed the list to the handful of the most interesting buyers. Being uninvolved in the selling process and being only partial owners of ColorMatrix stock, John and I suffered much less seller's anxiety the second time around. Then again, we did each still own almost 7 percent of the company. The three Europeans combined owned almost 7 percent, too. That made all five of us keenly interested in the sale.

CHAPTER 54

Gray

MIKE

By the second quarter of 2011, PolyOne had entered into exclusive due diligence with ColorMatrix. PolyOne was a publicly owned, $3 billion revenue specialty plastics company headquartered in Avon Lake, a leafy, lakeside suburb of Cleveland. Simultaneously, economies throughout Europe started to slide and China's economic growth began to soften. By 2010, the U.S. financial crisis, which had reared its ugly head in 2006, taken over most economic indicators by 2008, and continued to decimate the economy into 2009, was showing "green shoots"—tiny glimpses of improvement. Europe and China were a few years behind this curve. Their economic downturns, which had been minor in 2008 and 2009, became more acute in 2010 and 2011.

Before 2010, we had expected ColorMatrix to continue to grow in Europe and China. And, indeed, the company performed well in Europe for the first four or five months of 2011. Then its growth and profitability stalled. Given the economic situation in China, could our growth in that country follow suit?

This could be interesting, I thought.

Fortunately, ColorMatrix's growth recovered, and the investment bankers completed the process. On December 21, 2011, PolyOne Corporation acquired ColorMatrix for $486 million. The purchase price represented a more-than-2x revenue multiple and about 11 times annual EBITDA. These are robust purchase-price multiples. The three employees who had opted to roll their deferred compensation into equity cashed out very well, as did those to whom we had reallocated our stock options during the Audax recap.

For our part, John and I didn't have jobs for the first time since graduating from college in the mid- and late-1960s. We went to a deal-closing party that Dave McBride had organized at a steakhouse and looked around at the 75 people in the room. There were the Baird investment bankers and the Grace Matthews guys; Doug and John; our mentors—people like Arnold Coldiron and others; and longtime team members like John Standish, our research and development guru.

I couldn't eat, the moment was too emotional—no more ColorMatrix in my life.

"They're gonna run ColorMatrix differently from the way we did," John said. "I can already tell."

The folks at PolyOne would put their imprint on the company, making it their own. They probably wouldn't prioritize SALES FIRST! like John and I had. They likely would develop products first and then see if they could sell them—an order of events that never made sense to us because we sold first, then developed the product. It was a good thing we were out of the business.

"I wonder how the team will adapt," I said to John.

"I don't know."

He didn't say anything more. His silence said everything—we had zero control, so it didn't matter.

It was winter, the time when what locals call "the cloud" descends on Northeast Ohio. From November through April, our hometown is pretty gray, interrupted only by white when snowstorms careen into Cleveland.

But who was I to complain about the colorlessness all around? For so long, color had been pretty good to John and me.

Postscript

In a span of 50 years or more, plastic has become "too much of a good thing" in that too many people use too much of it. Despite this, we think it makes sense to develop a career in the polymers industry. Going forward, leaders have the opportunity and obligation to determine how to "lightweight," reduce, reuse, and recycle plastics more and more. We worked to do this with the technologies we licensed, which helped lightweight plastics and make more efficient use of them.

From 1967, when the movie *The Graduate* was released, in which a young man was advised to go into plastics, to today, when too much plastic pollutes the Earth, the world has changed. The lesson for our readers is that global needs will change during your careers—be prepared to lead change within your industry.

$$-\overset{\displaystyle H}{\underset{\displaystyle H}{C}}-\overset{H}{\underset{H}{C}}-\overset{H}{\underset{H}{C}}-\overset{H}{\underset{H}{C}}-\overset{H}{\underset{H}{C}}-\overset{H}{\underset{H}{C}}-\overset{H}{\underset{H}{C}}-\overset{H}{\underset{H}{C}}-$$

The partial chemical structure shown under Mike's name in chapter headings is a vinyl polymeric structure, related to polypropylene, a very widely used polymer. Liquid colorants are made by dispersing pigments in natural, un-colored vinyl polymers, then mixing it with plastics in a molding machine.

$$\left[-O-\overset{\displaystyle CH_3}{\underset{\displaystyle H}{C}}-\overset{\displaystyle O}{\overset{\|}{O}}- \right]_n$$

The chemical structure shown under John's name in chapter headings is the polyester structure for polylactic acid (PLA). ColorMatrix helped develop commercial applications for PLA for use in colorants, lubricants, and reheat additives.

About ...

JOHN HAUGH is a plainspoken business executive with big goals. He joined ColorMatrix in 1979 as its chief relationship builder, eventually creating SALES FIRST!, a basic, proven method of growing a company the old-fashioned way (by creating and selling solutions). John grew up in Minnesota and learned hard work, ambition, and egalitarianism from his parents.

MIKE SHAUGHNESSY learned everything he needed for success working as a chemical salesman for big companies, where mentors helped him become a top-notch business executive. When he eventually broke off to grow his own company, he came up with the vision for ColorMatrix and spent years leading the company's strategy and growth as president. After ColorMatrix, he and his late wife, Marian, a nurse, committed themselves to the cause of advancing nursing education.

 **BECCA BRAUN** is president of the Braun Collection, which creates and publishes memorable and adventurous stories for business enthusiasts. A critically acclaimed and bestselling writer and a guest lecturer in business classrooms, Becca believes in the positive power of business done well. She has written, ghostwritten, and coauthored hundreds of biographies, memoirs, adventure stories, travelogues, scripts, speeches, and articles. She is also a seasoned serial entrepreneur and business executive who earned an MBA from Harvard Business School. She has four children and lives with her husband in Cleveland, Ohio.

THE BRAUN COLLECTION is a suite of products that intimately acquaint business enthusiasts with business leaders across industries and geographies. Our True Business Adventure Tales®, comic books, and BizBio® CEO conversation cards deliver action-packed tales and visual stories. They go deep fast to uncover the lives, backgrounds, obstacles, opportunities, and best and worst ideas of the decision makers who have changed business. For coaches and educators, Braun Collection offers related tools, including teaching notes, videos, presentations, and live classroom lectures and video visits.

braun collection.

www.braunink.com/brauncollection

Check out other Braun Collection products, including:

True Business Adventure Tale® Books

Billion or Bust!: Growing a Tech Company in Texas

Comic Book Case Studies

Grit and Growth: Paul Schumacher and Schumacher Homes
Talk About a Bail Out!: Charlie Braun and Custom Rubber Corp.
Things Fall Apart: Rebecca Boenigk, Neutral Posture, and a
Crummy IPO
Exit Strategy: Linda Hall Leaves the Company She Loves

BizBio® CEO Conversation Cards

Jumbo Set (75 cards)
Full Set (50 cards)
Starter Set (25 cards)
Minority & Underrepresented
  Set
Immigrant & Foreign Business
  Set
Crisis Management, Turn-
  around, Covid-19 Set
Dealmaker, Restructurer Set

Entrepreneur, Founder, Innova-
  tor Set
Industrial, Agriculture, Utility,
  Conglomerate Set
Services, Media, Entertainment,
  Travel Set
Tech, Software, Biotech Set
Retail, Food, Beverage, CPG Set
Build-Your-Own Set

Teaching Tools

Teaching Notes
Quick Notes
Presentations
Video Shorts
Guest classroom lectures with Becca Braun
Live video classroom visits by authors and subjects of the books
and comic books